How (N

'An inspiration' Taylor Swift

'I was incredibly moved by Alex's story and her bravery
is second to none' Stephen Bartlett, entrepreneur
and host of *The Diary of a CEO*

'An amazing read. What a book.' Alex Jones, *The One Show*

'A real story of growth' Holly Willoughby, *This Morning*

'Such a powerful and raw story, honestly told'
Wes Streeting MP

'An inspirational read on the need for vulnerability in sport'
Women's Health

'A staggeringly open and exposing read' Suzy Wrack,
journalist for *The Guardian* and author of *A Woman's
Game: The rise, fall, and rise again of women's football*

'Painfully honest but also inspiring. Every young
girl who loves her football should read it' *Daily Star*

'Alex Scott is extraordinary' John Sutherland

'*How (Not) To Be Strong* chronicles Alex Scott's journey
from the East End to international football stardom and
broadcasting mainstay with candour and heart, revealing a
vulnerable side to the driven athlete that the public
seldom see' *Waterstones.com Sports Book of the Year*

'A searingly honest read, this book is an inspiring tale
of succeeding against the odds' *FourFourTwo Magazine*

ABOUT THE AUTHOR

Alex Scott MBE is an award-winning broadcaster and former professional footballer. She helped Arsenal in their historic 'quadruple' season, in which they won all of their trophy competitions, and was later appointed as the team's captain. She represented England in 140 appearances with the Lionesses, retiring as the second most-capped England player across the men's and women's game.

Alex is one of the UK's most in-demand presenters, appearing on *The One Show, Children in Need, Sport Relief* and ITV's *The Games*. In 2021, she made history as the first permanent female host of BBC's Football Focus. She is an ambassador for the BBC's mental health platform, Headspace, and holds honorary doctorates from the University of East London and University of Hertfordshire.

How (Not) To Be Strong

Alex Scott

PENGUIN BOOKS

PENGUIN BOOKS

UK | USA | Canada | Ireland | Australia
India | New Zealand | South Africa

Penguin Books is part of the Penguin Random House group of companies
whose addresses can be found at global.penguinrandomhouse.com

First published by Century 2022
Published in Penguin Books 2023
002

Typeset in 12.8/15.15pt Garamond MT Std by Jouve (UK), Milton Keynes
Printed and bound in Great Britain by Clays Ltd, Elcograf S.p.A.

The authorised representative in the EEA is Penguin Random House Ireland,
Morrison Chambers, 32 Nassau Street, Dublin D02 YH68

A CIP catalogue record for this book is available from the British Library.

ISBN: 978-1-529-15913-4

www.greenpenguin.co.uk

Penguin Random House is committed to a
sustainable future for our business, our readers
and our planet. This book is made from Forest
Stewardship Council® certified paper.

This book is dedicated to the dreamers.
It might not always feel like it, but you've got this!

As difficult as it may be, we have to reach a point where we let go of the burdens of our experiences and share the beauty of the lessons they left behind.

Morgan Richard Olivier

Contents

Introduction

Today, I am smiling. I think it's the first day in months when I've woken up and my brain is filled with colour, memories, moments, trains of thought. I can feel growth within myself once again. As I'm writing this, my head is clear. I feel like I'm back.

I don't know where the start, middle or end of this book is. What I do know is this: like most things in my life, how I go about writing it will probably not be in the way we are 'supposed' to do things. But I will 'trust the process', as they say. People have been asking me to write a book since I retired from football in 2018. I had meetings and spoke to people about the idea. Did I need the money? Hell, yes I did. But deep in my gut, it didn't feel right. As tempting as the offers were, my instinct was stronger. I just had a sense – one that has always seemed to be there for me during big life decisions – that there was more to that chapter of my story yet. I didn't have a clue what that could be, but I listened. Turns out, my instinct was correct. There was a lot more to come. And now the time is right.

I've been in a dark space for the last six months. What I have learned over the past couple of years is that I'm very good at disguising when I feel low, when my head is fogged. I've often wondered why this is, why I feel the need to always be strong. I feel very guilty about my sadness; from the outside looking in, what the heck do I have to be sad about? I've managed to have a successful career in two fields I am passionate about. But what's worse than feeling guilty about being sad is putting on a happy face, so that others think you're OK, especially when you can't articulate the emotions you're feeling in the first place; pretending to yourself that this is a form of strength. It messes with your head.

I feel as though I've saved up all my vulnerability and I'm letting it all out in this book. This is the real me. Don't get me wrong, I'm scared. But there's no going back now – and I'm also excited, at the thought of being free. I've carried such a lot of fear, of being judged, or of hurting other people if I speak my truth. And I hope that by showing you the lessons I've learned throughout my life – about what strength is and isn't – you might find some strength too.

Why is now the right time? Maybe because I'm learning how to be a little more selfish and to ask myself what *I* need first and foremost. And because there is a whole lot of stuff I need to get off my chest. If I continue not to speak about certain experiences that have shaped me and my beliefs, I feel like I'm being dishonest with you all – and myself.

My public persona is one of strength. I've managed to turn my pain into power. Some of you will have been on the journey with me all the way from the East End.

Some will have joined during my football career. Or maybe you just know me as 'Alex from the telly'. My life has been a full one, in so many different ways. And I've reached a point where I'm ready to look back on what has happened so far, to start making sense of it all and drawing those threads together. And I'm also ready to redefine what it means to be 'strong', to let my walls down and open up. Get ready; it's time to flip my fear.

'Don't ever let fear hold you back' is one of my favourite sayings. Well, let's do this, then.

I

Strength Is . . .
Knowing Where You Come From

The other day, my taxi driver started telling me stories, as people in that line of work like to do. He used to be a bus driver, he said, and at times would have to drive the 309 bus route. He hated the route, though, because it went through the Aberfeldy estate in Poplar, which has a reputation for being so rough that he didn't feel safe. What he didn't know was that Aberfeldy is my manor, and has been since my parents took me home from the hospital in October 1984. The driver had picked me up from Mayfair, a 'nice bit of town', and probably couldn't conceive of me ever having been near the area he was rubbishing. I didn't let on that I knew Aberfeldy, had spent my childhood there. I wanted to hear how others really viewed the little pocket of London where I grew up. 'Rough and not much life to it' is how the taxi driver described it.

It might be rough around the edges but there is a real sense of community in Aberfeldy; everyone knows each other and I've always felt safe. Around the estate, I was always 'Ronnie Scott's little sister' when I was growing up, which I didn't mind at all. It wasn't the prettiest place, with tower blocks situated in the centre of a busy triangle of main roads. On one side of the estate is the A12, always gridlocked during the morning and evening commutes. At the opposite end is the A13, filled with cars trying to escape the traffic of the Blackwall Tunnel or reach the motorway. Days were soundtracked by honking cars or the sirens of emergency services rushing somewhere.

I lived in a tall tower block with my mum, dad, brother Ronnie and about three hundred other people. We were at number 43 on the first floor, our door guarded by a black iron gate for extra protection, so no one could kick it in. The only play areas were a tiny patch of grass at the back of the tower block, or the waste land out front, situated by the gas works. It was ugly but it was my bedroom view. There were local shops and a school, but that was about it. Being able to get on with life and make the most of what you had was the way things were. That lifestyle gave me survival skills I carry with me to this day.

Growing up, my bedroom wall was plastered with posters of musicians that I would cut out from American music magazines. Everyone from Aaliyah to 2Pac was on that wall, but there were no sporting role models. My parents weren't massive sports fans, and we wouldn't sit down together and watch sport on the TV. I didn't have any dreams of being a footballer; I certainly didn't see any women footballers. The closest people I had to role models were the Williams sisters. From a young age, I think every Black child saw a reflection of themselves in the Williamses. They made mainstream news and transcended their sport from the very start because they didn't follow the same path as everyone else in their field; they did it their way and weren't afraid to show the world how and why. I read stories about how the sisters would train in caged tennis courts, with violence going on around them. They set an example and never relied on 'poor me' narratives; there was always pride in where they came from, and pride in the fact they'd trained so hard and made it. I think it allowed everyone in a similar situation to dream. I was proud of them. Every year I'd tune in to Wimbledon – I wasn't really a tennis fan at the time, but I wanted to watch *them* every year when they came to London. I would sit in front of the TV and dream that one day I'd go and see them play. 'If the Williamses can make it, no matter what, you can find a way to,' I used to tell myself. I imagined sitting in the green stalls of Centre Court, sipping on champagne and munching strawberries, just like I saw the rich white folk doing on my TV set.

Even though I don't live in Poplar anymore, it's still home. When I go to visit Mum and Ronnie, I love driving down the close and hearing neighbours like Catherine and Ann calling out my name to say hi, just like when I was a kid. I always look out for Rene down the street, to make sure she's OK and to give her a wave. Rene lived on the tenth floor of the tower block and would sit on her little balcony, shouting down to my brother and me on the patch of grass below with requests to go get cans of Irn-Bru for her from the local shop. We loved these missions because she'd always include an extra 20p for us to spend on pick 'n' mix. And Rene's daughter Avril served as our babysitter when Mum needed some help or would go on a night out. Then there's Sam, who works in the cafe I would stroll to every afternoon to get a tuna sandwich for lunch, and who still asks after me. Bee, in the off-licence. Mr Patel, who I remember rarely having conversations with, but come Eid every year, he'd always knock on our door bearing delicious food and a smile. These are the people who act as the anchors of my life, who ground me. It's my borough that made me who I am today.

My family has deep, deep roots in east London. I discovered this when doing *Who Do You Think You Are?*, the BBC's genealogy show, in 2021. I'd never asked many questions about my ancestors. Growing up, I was led to believe you don't ask questions; you wait until you're told. I went into *Who Do You Think You Are?* knowing very little, and everything they dig up on the show is presented to you for the first time on camera, so my surprised reactions were very real!

I discovered that we had Jewish roots on Mum's side, via my great-grandfather, Philip Gittleson, known as 'Philip G'. His parents had emigrated from Lithuania in the late 1900s to escape the pogroms. According to Mum, he was a total character – he'd even fought the fascists at the 1936 Battle of Cable Street. There's a mural in Wapping dedicated to the Cable Street skirmish that I used to walk past every time I visited Nanna Scott (my dad's mum), but until *Who Do You Think You Are?*, I didn't know anything about the event it represented. I'm proud that my family were fighting against hate even back then.

The historians uncovered other information that filled in some gaps. Philip G's brother Abraham – my grand-uncle – struggled with his mental health and ended up being sent to Colney Hatch Lunatic Asylum in 1934, when he was forty-one years old. Abraham lived there for thirty years until he died. I was heartbroken when I heard that; to think of him there, alone. I remember sitting on a hard park bench as I was being told this, trying to process it, with a camera in my face and being asked, 'Can you articulate the emotion you are feeling, Alex?' Honestly? Not really. The show is such a whirlwind; you're given so much information and barely have any time to wrap your head around it before it's on to the next part of filming.

Since the programme aired, I've tried to sort out everything in my head. I guess I feel a deeper connection, to both that part of my family and to a Jewish heritage I didn't even know existed. There's a sense of pride too, because my family fought for freedom and diversity in east London and I was a direct product of that. But their lives were full of sadness as well. I felt that deeply. It reminded me of how far we've come in even beginning to discuss poor mental health. When I was growing up, there was a place in east London called

St Clement's, and as kids we were told to stay away from it because it was inhabited by 'crazy people'. Infrastructure to support people with mental health issues may still not be as good as it could be in this country, especially if you haven't got money, but our understanding of the landscape has come on leaps and bounds in the last ten years alone.

Who Do You Think You Are? didn't just explore the history of my white ancestors. I finally went to Jamaica to learn more about the Scotts, my Nan's side of the family. It was my first time visiting the island – I'd always said I couldn't just go there on holiday; it's part of my history, and I wanted to know more about my family and who I was before I made the trip.

We filmed a few bits in London before heading off, which is when something interesting happened. See, in 2018, the actor Catherine Tyldesley, from *Coronation Street*, had arranged for me to see a psychic while we were touring with *Strictly Come Dancing*. We met in the Lowry Hotel, Salford, and I'll never forget what she told me that Friday morning. She said I would travel to Jamaica to find out more about my family, but also that Nan – who'd recently passed – had left me a ring which I hadn't been given. I hadn't known Nan had left me anything in her will. Don't worry though, the psychic assured me, because Nan was 'going to find a way to make sure I get it'. Three years later, I was filming the last of my UK segments for *Who Do You Think You Are?*, with my flight for Jamaica scheduled the next day. My cousin Marie had been showing me Nan and Grandad's Jamaican birth certificates, but as soon as we were done filming, she asked if she could have a minute to speak with me. I didn't really have time; I had to rush off as it was a photo-shoot day, I was running late to film Soccer Aid, and my brain was fried with the immense amount of information I was already trying to process about the Jewish side of my family. But I could tell there was something Marie really wanted to tell me off camera, so we went outside.

'I'm so sorry, Alex,' she said earnestly. 'I've got something that belongs to you. I've had it for a couple of years but I just can't keep it anymore. It's not meant for me, it's yours.'

As Marie put her hand in her pocket, I burst out crying.

She stopped and looked at me. 'Why are you crying?' she said.

'Is it a ring?' I asked, through tears.

She squinted at me, confused, but replied: 'Yes.'

By now, I was sobbing uncontrollably. It had happened just like the psychic said it would. The ring was Nan's wedding band, Marie told me. I threaded it on a thin chain and wore it for the rest of filming – if you watch the show back, in Jamaica, there I am, wearing Nan's ring around my neck. She was on the journey with me the whole time.

We managed to trace Nan's family all the way back to my great-great-great-great-grandfather, Robert Francis

Coombs. He was a light-skinned Black man who owned twenty-six enslaved people, a story that laid bare the complexities of enslavement. Lots of Black and mixed-race people actually participated in slave ownership – it was a way to gain status in the local community. It's something I don't think we hear about much because it complicates a lot of narratives for people, but at the end of the day, this was a way they thought they could survive – and even prosper – in a barbaric system created by white colonists. I hadn't really had time to think about how heavy it would be to learn so much about my family so quickly. I'd expected to discover my ancestors had been enslaved, but never the story that was now being presented to me. I kept thinking, 'How can someone own another's life?' Having to hear, and repeat, this information on camera is what makes the show, I suppose, but I'd forgotten this was a TV programme: it was my life and my family. For some reason my mum flashed into my head, and how she felt trapped in her life. The tears came rushing out. Robert Coombs was rare, in that he left provisions for an enslaved woman, Eleanor, and the children she bore him. But he still owned people. There's no getting away from that.

While visiting his grave in Jamaica, I met a local man who told me that everyone in the area was descended from Robert Coombs. He greeted me as a relative and told me: 'If you don't know where you're coming from, you don't know where you're going.'

He was right. I felt a part of me I didn't even realise was missing slot into place. It blows my mind to think that both sides of my family travelled so far, to pitch up in the same little patch of east London, just a stone's throw from one another. And that some of them were actively involved in the battle to ensure the diversity and freedom of the East End could prevail. It makes me even more proud to say I'm from the area; I'm an East Ender to my core.

But there's still people out there who think I should disown the traits that give away my roots. Growing up, when I watched TV, the presenters all looked, acted and spoke a certain way. Even the rare Black newsreaders seemed to have that cut-glass accent, like the one my friend Regan Coleman got after being sent to elocution lessons by her parents. I say 'newsreaders' because I can't really remember any other Black presenters growing up – only the likes of Andi Peters on kids' TV and Oprah, who Nan would let me watch with her.

I was even more conscious of my voice when I began broadcasting. And I quickly received confirmation that the way I spoke was not 'usual'. I remember getting detailed feedback after a work placement at Sky that said I would never make it as a presenter because my accent wasn't right. I was stunned. I read the message as I was coming up the escalator to catch the train home from London Bridge. It was one of those amazing days in the city where the sun was blazing and everyone seemed to be in a fantastic mood because of it. But my smile quickly sank into a frown. How could people in the industry fail to see that diverting from the 'usual' was a problem – for them! The lack of diversity on our screens was impacting quality; they *needed* different perspectives and voices. 'Well,' I thought, 'I'm not going to change. I'm gonna show them.'

Yet even when I began finding success as a presenter at the BBC, I was still on the receiving end of remarks about my accent. I remember talking to producers Louise Sutton and Steve Rudge, asking whether I should get elocution lessons to 'fit in'.

'No,' they both told me. 'People need to see you being you. It's a reflection of the UK that people have regional accents.'

They reminded me that I always say 'I am proud of where I come from', and that holding on to my accent was part of that. It would have been so easy to direct me to those lessons to keep others happy, but I'm grateful to Lou and Steve, who saw the importance of having voices like mine front and centre on a platform like the BBC.

In July 2021, I was named as part of the BBC's Olympic broadcasting team, an immensely proud moment. It was nearly ten years after I'd participated in the Games as an athlete (more on that later!) and felt like a real milestone in a completely new field. Still, I'll be real: it was the hardest broadcasting job I've ever done to date. The absolute graft needed to stay across every single sport, even events taking place throughout the night, coupled with dawn rises to interview the Olympians who've just won medals – the apparatus that goes into Olympics coverage is a non-stop machine. Actually being on screen for an hour and a half every night was the easy bit!

On 30 July, I'd just finished up the day's highlight show, presenting alongside Clare Balding. I was exhausted and, honestly, probably should have stayed offline altogether during that period – I was all too aware of the trolling I was most probably going to receive. Whatever I did on TV was met with racist and sexist messages on social media, ranging from overt discrimination to suggestions that I only got my job because I'm ticking some mythical 'diversity' box. But logging on briefly sometimes feels like an escape; I was spending all of my waking hours watching sport, talking about sport, and sometimes just ten minutes breaking out of my bubble at the end of the night reminded me the world outside was still there. Yet when I opened up Twitter, a tweet caught my eye. It was from a user with the name 'Lord Digby Jones', and as I processed what it said, I felt my stomach drop.

'Enough!' Lord Jones' post read. 'I can't stand it anymore! Alex Scott spoils a good presentational job on the BBC Olympics Team with her very noticeable inability to pronounce her "g"s at the end of a word. Competitors are NOT taking part, Alex, in the fencin, rowin, boxin, kayakin, weightliftin & swimmin.'

Trolling from anonymous accounts I had learned to brush past. But this wasn't trolling. This was a peer, slating my accent, slating *me* and my ability to do my job. It was exactly what I'd feared, going into the Games. I knew I was going to be judged every which way for who I was, and even more so given I was alongside a familiar and seasoned pro in Clare Balding, beloved by audiences. I'd put so much pressure on myself to not give those who wanted to see me fail any satisfaction. But here was something I couldn't – and didn't – want to change: my accent.

I sat on the sofa, reading the tweet over and over again. It was 11pm now and I was going back and forth in my head, debating with myself.

'Just ignore it.'

'No, I've bloody had enough!'

'Just forget about it.'

'Why me? Why can't people see I'm just trying to do my job to the best of my ability, that's all I'm doing.'

'Pour a glass of wine . . . forget about it . . . You have another show tomorrow, it's fine.'

'Nope, that's it . . . I've had enough of it. I'm proud of where I'm from.'

I started typing out a reply to Lord Jones. Then I stopped, and messaged Michelle Sultan, a renowned hair stylist I was working with. She was quite new in my life but was one of those people who feel like they've been there from the very beginning. From the moment I started working with Michelle, I knew she would tell me what she always thought, and not just what I wanted to hear. I trusted her. And she knew the industry like the back of her hand, while also coming from a similar background to me.

It was midnight now and I didn't expect a reply but Michelle was awake. We texted back and forth and she reiterated the advice I'd been given on previous occasions:

don't change for anyone. Michelle said she didn't think it would be a good idea to respond to Lord Jones. It would only give the tabloids more material and distract from the work I was doing. 'OK,' I typed back, and said goodnight.

But I couldn't stop thinking about it. I'd said I wouldn't reply to Lord Jones. The rule was not to add fuel to the fire. But this was burning away inside me, regardless. I was used to critique; this wasn't critique. It was classism, pure and simple, a personal attack on me and my upbringing. So I opened up Twitter and tapped out a response in three tweets, attaching a favourite quote from another Michelle, the former First Lady of the United States: 'When they go low, we go high.'

'I'm from a working class family in East London, Poplar, Tower Hamlets & I am PROUD,' I wrote. 'Proud of the young girl who overcame obstacles, and proud of my accent! It's me, it's my journey, my grit.'

In the final message, I posted an excerpt from one of my favourite Maya Angelou poems, having grown up with her writing and feeling it speak to me, like she was putting pen to paper about my life.

'You may shoot me with your words, you may cut me with your eyes, you may kill me with your hatefulness, but still, like air, I'll rise.'

I captioned the Angelou extract with a little sign-off just for Lord Jones: 'Tweets like this just give me the energy to keep going. See you tomorrow . . . live on BBC baby.'

Pressing 'send' felt good. Really good. Like I'd stood up for myself, instead of ignoring the disrespect as was my normal approach. And with that, I managed to put my phone down and snatch a few hours of sleep.

When I woke up, I'd forgotten about the events of the previous night. Then I saw a WhatsApp message from my manager, Sara.

'Have you seen the reaction?' she'd written.

Sleepily, I replied: 'Reaction to what?'

'Alex . . . your tweet.'

Oh, crap. Hastily, I sent Sara an apology, panicking about the fallout. But Sara's next message stopped me in my tracks.

'No, Alex, don't say sorry – have you seen the reaction of support for you?'

I hadn't even considered that part. Opening up Twitter, I found my notifications flooded, but not with abuse. Instead, people were sharing stories of discrimination they'd experienced thanks to their accents, how they'd been denied opportunities, jobs, mortgages. I couldn't believe what I was reading.

Then I spotted a reply to Lord Jones from Stephen Fry.

'You are everything linguists and true lovers of language despise,' Stephen had written. 'Also, since we're being picky, you are not "Lord Digby Jones", you are Digby, Lord Jones. There's a world of difference. But however you're titled, you disgrace the upper house with your misplaced snobbery.'

Months earlier, Stephen Fry had been a guest while I was presenting *The One Show*, promoting his new book, *Troy: The Siege of Troy Retold*. I'd read it beforehand to prepare and found it fascinating. When it was time for his appearance, I told him all about how much I'd enjoyed the book and how I'd travelled around Greece as a way to learn the history and educate myself in a different way because I'd struggled with the teaching styles at school. We had a great conversation – Stephen taught me about the area of London I was from, telling me stories I'd never heard. I was transfixed. I never once felt like I had to pretend I was something I wasn't, and he could see how interested I was in what he was saying. There's been plenty of times I've worried about how guests from certain backgrounds might be with me because of my imposter syndrome, and I never forgot how comfortable I felt with Stephen. So to see THE Stephen Fry defend me like that, against someone who was a lot closer to his world than I was . . . it meant everything. I cried, of course.

I was so sad, not just for me, but at the stories I was being sent of how people had been made to feel, just because of the way they spoke. And yet I still had to go to work. I headed to the production office. Even though my stomach was churning, I didn't want anyone to assume there was something wrong – it felt like this would be a sign of weakness, that I couldn't handle the negativity that comes with being front and centre on a TV show. I didn't think any of the producers would have seen what was going on. I'd told my then-publicist Charlotte that I wasn't prepared to do any interviews or issue a statement in response to the press requests that were streaming in. I'd said everything I needed to in my tweets.

Even though I was receiving an amazing outpouring of support, I still felt utterly deflated. Why was I putting myself through this? Was I even strong enough to keep fighting these trolls? I was tired and drained, with the added stress of knowing that now I also had to memorise which words would be coming up in the script with a 'g' on the end. I thought if I made any mistakes that evening, Lord Digby Jones would win. I was just so tired of being judged, for being Black, for being a woman, for what I wore, for where I came from, for how I sounded. It felt non-stop. The old adage was true: I had to work twice as hard just to be judged as 'OK'.

I managed to hold it together throughout the show. But just as I began to introduce the final segment, a round-up of events we hadn't broadcast coverage of yet, I realised the autocue had been changed. I felt a grin spread over my face as I read out my line: 'So far we've been runnin', ridin', shootin', scorin', swimmin' and puttin', but we've still got a lot of gold to uncover.'

The next day, a work colleague Paddy told me it had been him who changed my line. In his early years he'd gone through similar situations of being judged on his accent and said he knew exactly how it felt. Of course, everyone had known what was going on with me that day, I realised. And this was their way of showing support, of saying: 'Stay strong, remember who you are and where you come from, always.'

From Jamaica to Poplar, these places and these people are with me always.

2

Strength Is . . .
Finding Your Voice

I'm going to tell you something I've managed to hide for most of my life, and only a few people know about. It doesn't sound like a big deal written down, but for most of my early childhood I couldn't really talk. Throw in the fact that I'm very dyslexic and you'd think I would have run in the opposite direction from the broadcasting path I chose to follow after my footballing career. Yet now I'm on TV in front of millions and use my voice every single day.

Mum spotted something was up when I was very little. I was good as gold as a baby. I loved my playpen and Mum could leave me there for hours with my fireman's hat on. Occasionally, she'd hear a little call for 'Ma' or 'Da'. But, besides those two words, I wasn't trying to speak. Doctors told my worried mum that I was fine and that she should stop comparing my progress with my older brother's. But Mum said she knew – as mothers do – that I was struggling. Eventually the doctor decided to send me for a hearing test, and that showed I had trouble with my ears and adenoids (little lumps of tissue at the back of the nose). Mum actually tells this funny story about when I first had the grommets (small tubes inserted into the eardrum) at about three years old. I would ask for the bath tap to be turned down because the sound was too loud.

'Ma, ta to lou,' I would say. I still couldn't form whole words – translation: 'Mum, tap too loud.'

The grommets became an ongoing procedure. The next time I had to get them changed, Mum and I stayed in hospital overnight, ready for my operation the next day. I wasn't allowed any food or drink in preparation. Early the next morning, I went off to the playpen to await the call for surgery. When Mum came to fetch me, I sauntered up, chewing away. 'Alex, what have you got in your mouth?' she shouted. I looked up, puzzled, and said, 'Swats, Ma.' One of the kids had given me a sweet. which meant another day and night spent in the hospital waiting to get the grommets done. Mum said she couldn't be mad at me; I had such an innocent face and couldn't even communicate. How could she be angry?

Because my issues with speech weren't detected until I was around three or four, I'd already developed my own language based on the fragments I could hear. So I then had to spend lots of time in speech therapy trying to actually learn where words and sounds come from. When Mum was working a shift at a local pub, Nana Lil, my mum's mum, would take me to the health centre on Vallance Road, sandwiched between Shoreditch and Whitechapel. For hours I'd sit there with the speech specialist, as they tried to teach me how words were formed via learning games. 'Alex, back of the throat, K K K K.' I'd have to repeat the sounds, and if I was doing well, they'd praise me. Nana Lil was given homework games to pass on to my mum, so I'd spend evenings practising with her, too.

Being that young and carefree, I didn't really think much about what was going on and why I was being taken out of nursery to keep going to this other place. I was just happy to be holding Nana Lil's hand as we walked to our destination. One very sunny afternoon, it was boiling in the health centre when the fire alarm went off. Everyone inside was rushing around as we were escorted out of the building. I stood on the grass outside for what felt like forever and, for the first time, actually studied the building: tall, light brown brick, crowned with a pale green roof. I didn't have my lesson that day; we were sent home as they couldn't sort the fire alarm system out. When I got back, I excitedly tried to explain to 'Ma' what had happened. To me, what I was saying sounded completely normal, but I could tell from the look on her face that to her it sounded like gibberish. So I eventually fell silent, as I always did when it was easier than carrying on.

Eventually my speech therapy funding was reduced, so I ended up going only once a week. Which meant being in school more. I had started school a year late because of all the time I had to spend in speech therapy, which meant I was playing catch-up with the other kids.

It so happened that my new teacher Miss Tuffin's previous job had been in a school for children with speaking difficulties. And now here I was, in her class. It felt like she'd been sent from heaven.

Miss Tuffin was very tall, with a black curly bob. She was skinny; when I hugged her goodbye at the end of my school day, I would feel her bones and worry she didn't have enough food in her house. She quickly became the only teacher throughout all my school years who I thought was absolutely amazing, and who seemed to reflect the same affection back at me. Miss Tuffin never forced me to speak in class, or encouraged me to be loud like some of the other kids who were very confident at that age. Instead she let me stay in my own head and work things out. So as not to show me more affection than my classmates, Miss Tuffin would keep me for an extra thirty minutes to an hour at the end of the school day, teaching me how to speak through music. She'd sit at the piano, me perched on the leather seat beside her, and play different nursery rhymes, trying to get me to sing along. Her patience was endless; when she would see me in my head, not understanding where a certain letter or word came from, we'd repeat it over and over through music until I got it. Finally, I could sing nursery rhymes and would be the loudest kid in class belting them out, just so Miss Tuffin would hear me and I'd make her proud. Maybe that's where my love of music started, through Miss Tuffin.

To this day I still have a lisp, but you'll only hear it

when I'm tired. What you might spot is that my brain works faster than my mouth; I have all these thoughts that want to come spilling out but they get stuck, literally stuck. If you're watching TV closely when this happens, you might see my eyes widen – that's the point when the words are jammed. It takes me right back to those early years of having to learn where sounds come from again. However, on TV I don't have time to repeat words out loud to myself, so I pivot to either rewording what I'm saying or simplifying my thoughts. When you see me stumbling on certain words, it's because however many times I try, I just cannot say the word – so I have to change it.

Dan Walker spotted this in me when I started presenting alongside him. I would sit with him in the *Football Focus* studio and he would put questions to me: 'Alex, what do you make of Chelsea's performance this week?', and so on.

I'd start my analysis. I tend to talk rather fast to get all my words out, but when my words got stuck I'd slow down, look at Dan and stutter a little. He'd immediately understand and take back over or jump in with another question, allowing me the time to come up with a different word that I could say without hesitation. Dan is one of the most kind and generous broadcasters I've worked with.

I also found myself telling Clare Balding about my speech difficulties during our time together covering the 2020 Olympics, thanks to Lord Digby Jones. I revealed the lengths I went to in order to hide my impediment and memorise scripts because I can't always read the font on autocues. She was shocked and didn't have a clue, but as soon as I opened up, she instantly changed how we operated – rewording certain sentences to a different format so they would flow for me.

This was the first time I understood that hiding something is not always the best option. I'd always felt that I didn't want people to feel sorry for me or to help me out of pity, so I found myself doing everything I could to keep it a secret. In actual fact, those people knew the ways to make my job easier; they had a better process for me than the one I had put in place.

But secrecy as survival has been a big part of my life. It goes back to childhood, of course. Maybe this is the part where I talk about my dad. His shadow hangs over this book. But the thing is, he's not been present in my life for a long time.

Mum used to say I was a daddy's girl. And from what I can remember – after speech therapy got me forming whole words – I would always be shouting 'Daddy, Daddy, Daddy'. I've got videos of me chirping, 'Look, Daddy!' and dancing to records he would play. When Dad was sober, he was a charming guy; he had a real swag about him. But the moment drink was involved, that would all change.

I'm no expert on alcoholism. I can only speak about my experiences with people I've known who have had issues with drinking, of which there have been, sadly, many. Dad was the first. Every day, as evening closed in, he would give me and my brother a couple of pounds and we'd head to the off-licence to pick up Dad's usual. It was the same every time: a couple of cans of Strongbow and Foster's. Sounds so innocent, right? Like that's going to do anything to anyone. Well, every night we would see what it could do. Dad's character would change in front of us: his voice, his eyes. Depending on what headspace he was in, we would be walking on eggshells, praying that we would make it through the night without an 'episode'. I would lie awake in bed, tense and terrified, waiting to hear if Mum was OK, listening for any movement. Was that her going to the toilet? Or were those all-too-familiar thumps? Could I hear her cries? Or the pleas of 'Tony, please, no' before another blow landed?

Those noises will never leave me. Even thirty-odd years on, it's still so raw. I felt absolutely helpless; all I could do was lie there and pray my mum would be alive in the morning. Now, I wonder if my brother did the same thing. We've never spoken about it and I still don't think we'd be able to, even today – I'm crying as I write this because it hurts so deeply to go back there. None of us wants to remember. But we also can't forget. The thought of my dad reading this also makes me sad. I'm sorry to even be writing it. But I have to because it explains so many of the patterns that have shaped my life since – and how I have slowly learned to understand and speak about them.

Living in fear every day is a feeling I would not wish

on my worst enemy. I had a little escape in the form of my room. (I say 'my' room, but Dad was always quick to remind us that nothing was ours, it was all his.) Mum didn't even have that. In the fourteen years she was with my dad, she wasn't allowed to do anything without his permission. Her freedom was totally stripped from her.

Control was everything to my dad. If we ever went out for a family meal, we had to sit at the table and not say a word to anyone unless we were spoken to first. People would say, 'Oh, ain't they so well behaved?' about Ronnie and me, but we sat there in fear. For us, going out for dinner wasn't a treat, it was an act of playing happy families. My brother and I did as we were told because we knew what would happen to us later if we didn't. I would sit and count how many drinks my dad was having, trying to judge if his eyes were glazing over, playing scenarios in my head of how I could try and save Mum that night. Some of the things my dad did seem so ridiculous in retrospect, but at the time they had us frozen in fear. That's abuse – escalating and arbitrary, just so the person calling the shots can flex how much power they hold.

One episode I'm reminded of daily, thanks to a red mini-skateboard that lives in my house. My brother and I were playing football downstairs on the little grassy area outside our tower block and the whole block could see who was on the green by looking out of their window. Dad always told us we must never leave that green, and we didn't – until the ball we were playing with rolled across the side street next to it. Normally when this happened we would get someone walking by to throw the ball back, but that day no one passed our way. My brother kept looking up at one particular window on the first floor of the tower block – to where Dad would peer out and see what we were up to.

'I think we're in the clear,' my brother whispered, before sprinting across the road, quick as a whip, to fetch the ball. We only managed a couple of touches before a voice boomed, 'RONNIE! ALEX! GET UP HERE NOW!'

Our heads dropped. We thought we knew what was in store, but Dad had an extra surprise for us that day. When we reached our flat, Dad spoke in his familiar, dangerously low, icy tone: 'I told you, you're not allowed to leave the green.'

'But Daddy—' I said, before: THUMP. The beating came hard and fast. Ronnie started shouting, 'No, Dad, not her, hit me!'

'Oh,' said Dad, rounding on him, 'you think you're a big man, trying to protect your sister?' Then he was hitting Ronnie too.

This went on for a while, but just when we thought the punishment was over, he straightened up. 'Right,' he said. 'Go and get all your toys and throw them down the chute.'

I heard my mum's voice then, pleading, 'Tony . . .'

'Shut up or you'll be next,' he told her.

My brother and I were marched down the passageway

from our rooms to the balcony, back and forth, with armfuls of our toys. Dad watched as we tearfully pushed each one into the garbage chute.

'Is that everything?' he said, after several trips.

I looked at the floor.

'Well?'

I wonder now why I didn't just stay quiet. But little Alex felt too guilty at the thought of hiding the truth.

'No, Daddy,' I whispered.

'What do you have left?' he said, softly.

'Ma skateboar,' I snuffled, speech impediment coming out.

This skateboard was my favourite thing. It was miniature and red. I couldn't use it properly; my knees would be constantly marked with scrapes and bruises from where I would scoot around on it. But I loved that skateboard. In my head it wasn't a toy.

'Go and get it,' Dad instructed.

I wept as I pushed my little red skateboard into the rubbish. And just like that, it was gone.

Years later, I told this story to one of my partners, who was so moved that they got me a replica. The thought was touching; I know all they wanted was to recreate that feeling of being a kid with her childhood skateboard, but in reality the skateboard just reminds me of my dad's abuse, and I dodge telling people the true meaning behind it when they come round to my house. As soon as visitors come in and see this baby skateboard, they laugh. 'I didn't know you were into skateboarding,

Al,' they say. I'll laugh back and say something about it being a toy from years ago I've not got round to chucking, then move the conversation quickly on.

Now, writing it all down feels like a catharsis. I'm still not sure I'm ready to throw the skateboard away just yet; it's a reminder that I'm in control of its fate now, not him. So maybe it'll stick around a bit longer.

Another memory that illustrates just how controlled our lives were was the time Dad bought a camcorder. He loved all things new, like cars and tech – it made him feel special and cool. It's why to this day I have no interest in BMWs, as they were his favourite. When Dad got his camcorder they were the flashy new thing, massive pieces of tech that had to sit on your shoulder because they were so big. And he decided the best way to test it out was on his kids. He ordered a Chinese and made Mum go with him to pick it up. Before he left, he set up the camcorder and beckoned Ronnie and me over to the sofa. Then he instructed us that we couldn't move until he and Mum got back. Mum gave us her 'look', full of love and helplessness. We understood it perfectly. It said, 'Please, just do as he says so there's no physical pain this evening.'

As they walked out the door, Dad told us the rules one more time: 'Do NOT move!'

So we didn't. When they got back, Mum thought there was something wrong with the video because we were so scared we barely blinked. I'm laughing typing this because it's so stupidly cruel. I'm pretty sure it was retribution for an incident that had happened earlier that week, where my brother and I had been ordered not to move but were caught playing a game of 'You Can't Touch The Floor Because The Crocodiles Will Eat You'. We'd already received a beating for that, but apparently this was dessert.

Two other episodes stand out for me, of life before my dad left. One is the first birthday party me and my brother ever had. The other is the day Dad actually walked out the door.

I was six and my brother was eight when we somehow were allowed to have a joint birthday party at the community centre across the road. All our neighbours and most of the adults in the tower block came down. Oh my goodness, the fun we had! I had the best time dancing with Mum; she looked radiant and happy. When allowed, Mum was the life and soul of the party. People love my mum – she has this special spirit about her. I heard the beginning of 'Hold On' by En Vogue blasting through the speakers and my mum's voice ringing out, 'ALEX!', beckoning me to come and join her. This was mine and Mum's song. Even though I was six, I knew every word and sang it with the same pain I heard in the song, holding my little finger up while delivering lines like 'Oh, my first mistake was . . .' Mum and I were in the middle of a circle of people watching us dance and perform.

Eventually everyone ended up at our flat to carry on the party. Dad asked Mum to go and get some lemonade and I stiffened – I could hear that certain tone in his voice and just knew Mum was in for trouble. Mum, perhaps buoyed by the joy of the party, replied that she was in the middle of a conversation with her friend. Dad asked her again.

'Tony, you can just go quickly and grab it,' Mum laughed. She didn't seem to realise the danger she was in – or maybe she did, but with a few drinks inside her, she had some liquid courage. Dad stomped off and got it. But when everyone left, the horror began.

I will never get the image of my mum running down the hall, screaming for help, out of my head. Hearing Dad drag her back along the passage, I had tears streaming down my face, my fists clenched. 'Why don't I just run across the passage and punch him?' I asked myself. But my body was frozen in fear. The noises were the worst I'd ever heard. I began crying more, thinking that he had killed her. All night I lay there, rigid, not being able to move until morning came and I could get out of bed without Dad telling me off.

Finally, the ordeal was over. Mum was still alive. Her face showed only part of what we knew had gone on; it was that battered even I was scared to make eye contact with her. The rest was covered by her clothes. But every time she tried to move, I could see the pain she was in. Mum, I'm sorry I couldn't save you. Truth is, after that evening, you saved Ronnie and me. You found an inner strength and gave us freedom.

Not long after, Dad was gone. Mum swears losing

Nana Lil to a sudden heart attack gave her the voice to tell my dad, finally, to fuck off. I was eight and I remember the day well. 'Alex, Ronnie, get in here,' Dad called from their bedroom. It was early afternoon; sunlight trickled through the windows. We stood in the hallway, while Mum sat on the bed, hiding her face, all battered and bruised. I wanted to run and hug her but I knew it wasn't allowed or, worse, could provoke another episode.

'Do you want to live with her?' he said, sternly. 'Or me?'

Despite everything my dad had done to us, this tore my heart out. I could see the good in him; it was the drink that brought out his worst qualities. I prayed every night that he was going to be OK, and thought that if I showed him all the love I could, he would love us back. But despite being a daddy's girl, the answer was only ever going to be Mum. And just like that, Dad was off – and he made sure he took everything.

At least, he physically left. But he didn't really leave because the pain was still there. You can put a plaster over a wound but if you don't treat it, it's going to fester. As a three – Mum, my brother and me – we never really dealt with it. I often wonder if he feels any guilt about leaving or if he's actually over it and has accepted the fact he chose to walk away. We were left with nothing, materially and financially. But we still had the three of us, a mother's love and a newfound strength. Finally, we could start to get our voices back.

There was still on-off contact for a while. When I was

twelve, we were struggling big time for money. I needed a new pair of football boots because mine had holes in them. The only thing for it was to get on the phone and ask Dad for £20 to buy some Puma Kings. Picking up the receiver, my voice completely faltered and the fear rushed in; most of the conversation on my end was 'Yes, Dad', 'No, Dad' and 'Thank you, Dad'. I managed to squeak out my request and he said he'd call me back with an answer. When he did, it wasn't good news. He'd talked to his new girlfriend, he said.

'Girls shouldn't be playing football so we don't believe that the money will be put to good use,' he told me.

My response?

'OK, Dad, thank you, Dad, talk soon. Love you.' After that, Mum made a promise to me and Ronnie that we'd never again have to ask for anything from my dad. And we didn't. Despite this, I tried to continue to be in my dad's life until 2017, sending him Christmas cards, birthday cards and presents. There was never anything in return.

I've never spoken about this side of my dad publicly. I've always been scared that if I talked about my childhood, I would ruin his life. My mind would go to dark places: what if he lost his job? His friends? Then he would drink more. What if he died, and it was the result of me speaking about the environment my brother and I grew up in? Now I'm wondering, what if he reads this? That won't be nice for him, will it?

It feels so odd to still be trying to protect his feelings.

But that's what abuse conditions you to do. Protect the perpetrator. When I think about it, I'm thrown right back into the emotional turmoil of little Alex, living in fear of doing or saying the wrong thing. One wrong look could result in a huge and terrifying reaction. All I wanted was that security you are supposed to get from parents: the hugs, the warmth, that safe feeling.

As I bring this chapter to a close, I want to ask one thing: please don't judge my dad for his past actions. Those that know him today and might be reading this, take him as he is now. I don't want him to be judged on who he was then. I have no hate towards him at all, just sadness when I think of what might cross his mind if his thoughts ever stray to our shared past. I hope he has healed. Sharing this story is not an attempt to hurt or punish him; it's me letting go of the past in order to dream of the future.

I've spent many years in silence, whether at the hands of others or self-imposed. It took me years to find my voice; it's going to take more still to raise it up, to make up for all those years it was quiet. But this book is me, talking straight to you, uncensored. This book is my voice.

3
Strength Is . . .
Defying Expectations

Before there was Highbury Stadium, there were jumpers for goalposts on the little green verge outside our tower block. And on the days we were allowed to venture further afield, there was a concrete football cage at the heart of the estate where I played with my brother and the other kids from a young age. There was no thought to it; it was just the game of choice. So my sporting career began by being plucked from the football cages of east London, literally.

One weekend in the summer holidays when I was about seven or eight, there was a five-a-side football tournament organised only a stone's throw from the estate. Anyone who lived in Tower Hamlets could enter. Events like this always took place in the holiday period to help families like mine; it meant the kids were out of the house all day and parents knew they were safe and staying out of mischief. I was furious, though, because Ronnie and his friends had entered a team and I wasn't in it. I spent the days leading up to the tournament sulking, refusing to speak to him. I always played with the boys in the football cage! Why leave me out now?

Looking back, it was fair enough; my brother wanted it to be just him and his boys. He couldn't always have his little sister hanging around. But at the time, I was *mad*. The Saturday morning of the tournament, however, Ronnie shouted down the flat hallway, 'Alex! We need you to play. Ricardo is ill so you're coming with us.' I'd got the call up! I jumped out of bed and threw on my trainers, with a huge grin plastered across my face.

Arriving, it felt like every kid in Tower Hamlets had turned up. There were only two pitches, which meant two matches at any one time, watched by dozens of beady little eyes. This was my first real experience of playing football in front of a crowd. I was able to keep up with all the boys; I was fast and hours of playing with the estate boys in our football cage meant I knew how to be physical and hold my own. Even though Ronnie was my big bro, I'd never had any special treatment – I had to fight for my place every time I entered that cage (and am forever grateful for it).

We got knocked out in the quarter-finals and were absolutely gutted, but plonked ourselves down to sit in the blazing sun and watch the rest of the tournament unfold. Suddenly a shadow blocked the sun; I looked up to see a man standing in front of us.

'Hi,' he said. 'I'm Edwin Lewis, I've been reffing some of the games today. I know some people at Arsenal and

I really think you should go down and have a trial. They have a women's team that you can join.'

I looked at Ronnie, then back at Edwin.

'Thank you,' I said. 'But I'm fine in the football cage with my brother.'

Edwin didn't move. 'Do you know there are women's teams you can play in?' he repeated.

The sun was beating down. I was more interested in drinking my Capri Sun that my mum had packed as a treat, than this man and his football team.

'I'm going to give you my card,' Edwin said, carefully. 'Please give it to your parents. You have something about you. I'm going to speak to Arsenal for you.'

I took the card from him and promised it would get to my mum.

When the tournament wrapped, we headed home. I was buzzing that I'd been able to play and had had such a fun time. Ronnie and I bounced through the door, excitedly recounting our day. Almost as a throwaway, I pulled out the card Edwin had given me and handed it over, not thinking anything of it. I certainly didn't expect to see him again but, later, my mum called him and the two of them agreed that I would go for a trial. From that point on, Edwin became a fixture. It turned out he was a youth worker in the area, who did so much for the kids in the borough. And true to his word, he organised a trial for me with Arsenal Ladies' youth team.

One weekend, Edwin took me up to Highbury, where

the youth squad trained. It was the first time I'd seen so many girls in one place, playing football. I was used to being either the only girl among boys, or one of two. But there were no boys here in the JVC Training Centre, and no concrete either – it was all sponge astroturf. We were split into small teams, handed bibs and told to start playing. From a small, open balcony above, parents were spectating. I'd never seen anything like it; it was fascinating.

Then the whistle blew and I snapped out of what felt like a daydream and into football mode. At the end, Edwin came back over to escort me home. I was super shy and wouldn't talk much unless spoken to – I had no idea how to ask questions or lead a conversation. But Edwin would comfortably natter on and on to cover my silence. To this day I'm not sure of the exact process of joining Arsenal – there was no big announcement – but they liked what they saw. I found myself making regular trips to the JVC Centre and was officially signed to Arsenal's youth team.

At the time I knew nothing about women's football, but it was great – I was making friends with all these kids from different backgrounds, learning so much about life outside Poplar. My curiosity about the world was being fed and only growing more rampant as a result. While I grew up in Poplar, I always say Arsenal is my home. From the age of eight, when I first signed for the club, it's been a steady family environment for me.

Training was in the evenings, twice a week. At this

point, I was struggling at school, which caused me a lot of anxiety. Miss Tuffin was long gone, and none of the other teachers understood me. It's not like I was troublesome; I would never dare to backchat teachers, but I had really bad communication problems. I dreaded English class. The school bell would ring to signal the end of break, and everyone would rush up the stairs like a herd of animals. I'd be bringing up the rear, internally panicking at the thought of the lesson to come. It always required some form of reading out loud; I'd pray the teacher wouldn't point their finger at me, breathing a sigh of relief every time I was given a reprieve. But sometimes I would be chosen and start sweating, looking round at my peers before silently shaking my head to make the teacher aware I wasn't going to do it. If only Miss Tuffin had been there; if only there'd been an understanding of what was going on in my head . . . But she wasn't there and I couldn't explain, so this little performance was seen as a disobedient rebellion. The whole process made me feel awful. In the 1990s, school was very one-size-fits-all; if you didn't fit the mould, it was your fault and you were seen as difficult. If only they'd known – I was crying out for help.

The easiest way for me to alleviate the anxiety school gave me was to simply not go most of the time. Some days I would head off to school, but then an incident would trigger my communication and speech issues and set off my anxiety, and all I could think about was getting to lunchtime when there was a clear exit route. Some of the kids were allowed home for lunch and had permission letters saying so. As soon as the lunch bell went, I developed a knack for reaching the school gate before the teachers who would stand there and check the letters, walking out full of confidence and with the freedom of knowing I would not be coming back to school that day.

On the days I didn't go in at all I would ride my bike down to Nanna Scott's and spend my days with her, trotting alongside her on the daily excursion to fetch the newspapers. Nan and I didn't really speak much about why I was choosing to spend my time with her, rather than at school. Maybe she knew I needed to be taught differently to the methods used within the education system. She certainly saw my willingness to learn from her. Nan would lay out all the broadsheets and tabloids and then we would sit together, reading the newspapers back to front. While doing this, she'd talk to me, telling me stories about Jamaica and her childhood there, or go off about something she'd just read on a front page. Nan would also encourage me to tell her what I'd just read and we'd discuss it together, which would always result in one of her old Jamaican proverbs.

'Ally-opps,' she would say. 'Likkle bud carry seed far.' Translation: A little bird takes a seed very far.

I'd look at her, confused.

'I don't understand, Nan.'

She'd then explain the meaning: a small effort can make a big difference in life. I loved all the Jamaican proverbs that she would use to explain stories to me.

'Talk and taste your tongue,' Nan would say as we sat and watched *Oprah*, her favourite show. It meant 'think before you speak'. Sometimes Nan would let me pick a horse from the newspaper and we would head out across the road to the betting shop. She always had a bet, just £1 or £2 a time, but she enjoyed a flutter. On the way to the shop, passers-by would shout out 'Hello Miss Scott!', which Nan would acknowledge with a nod of her head, while I'd raise them a smile beside her. She was a proud woman.

On Arsenal training nights I'd leave Nan's and jump on the 277 bus that took me all the way from Poplar to Highbury Corner. The team didn't know about my background. At football I was free from everything. It was *my* thing, separate from life outside. Most of the other girls often had both parents present at training sessions, but this didn't bother me. I knew Mum loved me and that she couldn't be there precisely because of that – she was working to get those football boots that Dad wouldn't pay for. Mum's friends would ask, 'What does Alex want to do when she's older?' Mum would proudly say, 'Oh, she wants to play football.' Her friends would laugh and reply, 'OK, but what *else*?' But Mum saw how much happiness and structure football was bringing to my life. Among so much else, I'll always be so grateful to her for letting me stick with it. It would have been easy to try and guide me towards another path or change my focus to education, but she allowed me to just be and to follow my passion.

From the moment I joined Arsenal, I knew this was a team that cared about winning. Nowadays, you're supposed to pretend that it's 'only the taking part that counts'. I'm glad that wasn't the attitude when I was young and playing because I don't think I'd have been able to tap into the drive and mindset needed to reach an elite level. Some people like Edwin would tell you I had raw talent, but when you're in an environment that demands the results from you as well, it's easier to keep striving for the top. We wanted to *win*. And we did – most weekends in the youth team, we'd win our games. With grace. It was an ethos drilled into us that we shouldn't brag or boast in consideration of the other teams. But god, was it a good feeling to win and lift a trophy. I was always a player that loved winning and loved the work that went into it – I lived for training. Perhaps because it was an escape for me, the sheer graft was something I fed off: running hard in fitness drills, darting about in agility training, the rush of endorphins and fulfilment when we'd finished.

Some of the parents of my teammates played a big part in supporting us. Sandra, who was the mum of our goalkeeper, Clare, and another single mum, lived ten minutes from Highbury and said I was welcome to stay with her whenever I needed to, and that she could take me back and forth to football.

Those days in the youth team were so special – compared to my life before, it felt like I didn't have a care in the world. We were travelling up and down the country, packed on to a minibus, and beating almost every other team we played. I made some amazing friends and was soon made captain of the Under-10s. This trend continued, and as I progressed through the age groups of U10s, U12s and U14s Arsenal Ladies, I became the go-to captain at every stage. There wasn't a big announcement that accompanied the role, but for someone struggling so much with school and her speech, to be put in a position of leadership felt huge. I had been at the club since the age of eight, so it was partly due to growing up with Arsenal, but I also had a way of welcoming new girls into the group. Away from football, I didn't have this big personality, but within that environment, I had the presence of a leader who could connect people. I knew the captain's armband came with the responsibility of leading by example and always trying to have a good game. The armband wasn't about me; it was about educating the rest of the players on the importance of what it meant to play for Arsenal, as well as bringing the squad together. Without reading any books on leadership or anyone officially telling me that this was my role, I understood.

There were a number of players I had particularly special bonds with back then. Like Ellen Maggs, who was going to be the biggest name in women's football – everyone at Arsenal would talk about Ellen being the next Kelly Smith or Marieanne Spacey, but to me, 'Maggsy' was just my mate. On the way home from matches, Ellen's dad Terry would always get us

McDonalds, which felt like such a treat because no way could my mum afford to be getting us that kind of food.

By the time I was playing for the U16s, a new signing called Regan Coleman had joined Arsenal from Ridgeway Rovers. Regan went to private school and was so different to anyone I'd ever met in my life – yet we instantly became best friends and still are to this day. Regan's house became a home-away-from-home for me, but it was a shock the first time I rocked up there. She lived in a big house in Chigwell with a garden and I'd seen nothing like it before – I was used to flats and council estates! Me and Regan were inseparable. I would stay at Regan's while she would troop off to school, and I would be there when she returned home. Regan's house was so large, I was afraid to be left alone while she was at school, so I would head downstairs when she was leaving and stay in the front room, watching TV and counting the moments until my best friend was back. It wasn't like I enjoyed those hours per se; I wouldn't eat, and every time there was a sound, I was worried someone had broken into the house. But all was forgotten the moment Regan returned. She'd tell me about her day at school and we'd head into the garden, playing football and badminton for hours, having so much fun, then go back inside to crowd round the table for dinner with her mum and dad. When I was staying overnight at Regan's, I'd call Mum back at home – there's not a day in my life I don't speak to my mum, even if it's just a hello – and tell her stories about my stay, like how amazing the toast was.

'They have posh bread, Mum!' I'd recount excitedly. The posh bread was from Greggs but it tasted better than any bread I'd had up until that point in my life.

When I was fifteen, I went with Regan's family to the Dominican Republic. While there, Regan even braided her hair so she could be like me, something we still laugh about to this day. I was teaching her to care for her hair the way Nan had taught me: that you have to grease your scalp so it's not dry, and deep condition your hair. We were so innocent to the fact that my Black Afro hair was very different to white hair. Whereas the deep conditioning made my hair look shiny, Regan ended up looking like one big greaseball. At the airport, Regan's mum and dad had to answer questions from border control because what was this middle-class white family doing with this Black kid? They thought her family was trying to smuggle me home with them. Regan's mum, Denise, laughed about it with me afterwards, but I remember feeling confused. I'd experienced overt racism before – when I was playing football, parents of opposing sides would yell the n-word at me or shout aggressively about the 'Black girl'. But not this surprising, sneaky racism. Yet as with most things, I never spoke about how it made me feel and just moved on.

For as much as Regan opened up worlds for me, she always says I did the same for her. I was her first Black friend, her first friend outside her white middle-class bubble. Despite living in London her whole life, she'd never been on a night bus or even the London

Underground, which I couldn't believe. 'How can anyone who lives in London not go on the tube?' I thought. But when you come from a world where your parents can drive you everywhere, I suppose you don't even think about it. The first time she stayed over at our flat, we were settling down on the sofa when there was a big commotion outside. We both rushed to the balcony and peered down below, to see a car alight and all the neighbourhood kids crowding round. The place was crawling with police officers and fire crews. The look on Regan's face was a picture! I could see how scared she was, so we took her back inside to watch TV and made some jokes.

The peace didn't last for long though; we soon had to call my mum because the TV was running out of minutes; she needed to put a pound in the meter. Thankfully she found one – it was the worst when we were in the middle of watching something and Mum didn't have a spare quid to put in the TV slot. Imagine being halfway through the last episode of *Euphoria* and the TV switches off. In those days, there was no catch-up TV either.

Regan rang her mum at the end of the sleepover, recalling the night's events in awe. She'd never seen anything like it. Even though my area was undeniably pretty crime-ridden and certain people on our youth team had negative perceptions of me as a result, she's always said there was not one moment she didn't feel safe when round at ours. My friendship with Regan really highlighted how home life under my dad had impacted our family. We grew up not allowed to hug or say 'I love you'.

While we would always kiss Mum on the cheek to say 'goodnight', we had to ask Dad before doing the same to him. Yet Regan's family were openly loving, which was nice to see but at the same time made me so uncomfortable. Regan still laughs about how I'd tense up when she'd go to hug me. I would stand there, not knowing what to do.

Regan wasn't my only mate, of course. I still hung about with the kids I'd grown up with in Aberfeldy. My friendship with Lea Reid – who everyone called 'Lea Girl' – highlighted how I found it easier to communicate through writing instead of speaking. Even though we lived down the road from one another, Lea and I would write each other letters all the time. So if I'd been at Regan's or away with football, we'd fill each other in on life events and what we were feeling in letter form. Even when we'd see each other every few days, Lea and I would exchange letters, documenting how we felt that day, and if we had any frustrations going on at home. We'd also express how much our friendship meant to each other. When we next hung out, strangely, we'd never mention what we'd said in the letters. We'd just continue as normal. They were our secret venting space.

When I wasn't with Lea Girl – who went to a different school and was a few years older than me – I would meet my friends Caroline and Denisha after they got home. Caroline lived two minutes from me but was classed as being from the Teviot estate, whereas Denisha was seen as a 'Bow girl' as that's where her estate was.

It's funny; now where you're seen to come from is attached to postcodes, but back then it was based on your specific estate. We'd jump on the DLR and head to Bow. There was a particular chicken shop there that attracted a young crowd. We'd grab chicken and chips, then stand on the street, hanging out, laughing about life. There wasn't really much to do, it was just a place for local teenagers to be young and free. On rare occasions, someone's 'crib' or 'yard' would be free as their mum would be out to work that evening, so we'd go and 'cotch' in the house. I always felt uncomfortable going to someone's house when their parents were away and clueless about it. I knew it was something we weren't really meant to be doing and I was actually quite a goody-goody, thanks to having the 'Arsenal values' drilled into me from a young age. Everyone in the manor knew I was playing for Arsenal, and I was scared that if I was ever caught doing anything wrong, it would get back to my coaches and jeopardise what I had there.

I hung out in places like pirate radio stations, where drink and weed were flowing freely, but I had no problem saying no. That discipline came from a fear of it affecting my football; my friends never pressured me to partake either, because they knew how important Arsenal was to me. I still loved being round them; the rigid structures of my footballing world were so far removed from the 'realness' of the East End, so hanging out with friends like Dylan Mills, now better known as Dizzee Rascal, kept me grounded. Dizzee would be spitting bars, constantly creating, getting gassed when he came up with new beats. When I've had conversations with Dizzee over the last couple of years, he always tells me how different and focused I was at that age.

'It's hard to explain,' he'll say. 'Everyone just knew to let you do your thing.'

Apparently I had this presence about me – but when I try to get him to elaborate, he laughs.

'Nah, I can't, all the man just knew you were a different chick,' he says. Then I laugh too. I've got no idea how to take that comment.

I suppose that growing up in the footballing environment continued to entrench some of those ingrained belief systems that my dad had first pressed on us (although more positively, for the most part). At football you don't show emotion, you're tough, you get on with things. You don't talk about stuff, you roll your socks up and do your best. This, combined with my communication problems, and some of the pre-formed judgements coaches seemed to have of me because of my background, could cause problems. Aged fifteen, I was nearly kicked out of the Arsenal youth team after our first trip abroad to play in the San Diego Cup.

This trip was a big event; it was our first time going abroad with the club and we'd spent many evenings standing at the end of supermarket tills with our Arsenal Girls buckets, fundraising in order to make it happen. Finally, we were on our way to play in this international tournament and test ourselves against American teams. We knew it was a huge deal to be representing Arsenal abroad. Our coaches were talking about going to watch a game featuring Kelly Smith, a former player whose team was part of the Women's United Soccer Association, the world's first football league in which women were professionals and paid wages to match. At fifteen, I didn't really know anything about international women's football – I was only focused on Arsenal and the U16s. The trip flew by; we had to pack everything in, with games over consecutive days, which meant ensuring our kit was all washed and good to go on the days we would be on the pitch.

The American heat was like nothing we'd ever experienced before, and playing at such a fast pace opened our eyes to how far behind our squad's fitness levels were. We didn't even make it through to the semi-final. As a youth team, we were the best in the UK, and crashing out of the San Diego Cup hurt. Some players were all right with it but I was in pain. We'd come to win! I couldn't be all smiles and cheers. The evening we lost our match, all I wanted was a flight straight back to the UK, so I could curl up at home with Mum. Things quickly got worse. I can't remember the exact offending incident, but it involved the washing of the team kit and something happening with the U14s team. I think somebody was accused of bullying. As a result, the entire U16 squad got into trouble and everyone was made to say sorry by the coaches. Having been through similar situations as a kid, I found this impossible. I was being made to say sorry for something I had played no part in. Why would I say sorry for the sake of it? My words were already limited, I had no interest in wasting them on something I didn't mean. The whole situation seemed hugely unfair on all the girls who'd been so good during the trip, and who were now being punished and sent back to the hotel early on the only night we'd been allowed to go 'out' for dinner. Every time I was instructed to say sorry, I shook my head.

'Alex, say sorry,' my coach, Clare Wheatley, told me sharply. I just shook my head again, equally frustrated, both with her and myself, for not being able to explain what was going on in my head. Suddenly, it was like I was back in front of my dad, bursting with the need to explain, yet knowing I wasn't allowed to, that you can't ever speak back to adults, you just say 'Yes, Dad' or 'No, Dad'. I kept shaking my head.

'That's enough,' Clare said, dismissing me. 'We'll deal with this when we get back to England.' Now we were both angry. I was deeply hurt by the situation because I knew that what had really happened was not how it had been presented by the coaches. Yet I couldn't find a way to communicate this. Instead, I bottled everything up and shut down – which was taken as evidence that I had a bad attitude and thought I was bigger than the rest of the team. I was Alex, who didn't go to school and just stayed round Clare's or Regan's. I could feel the weight of these judgements placed on me, the expectation that I wasn't going to do much in my life because it's not like

I was about to get good school grades. Recognising this misreading of me made all the anger and sadness I was carrying worse. We flew back to England the next day. As we pulled up outside Highbury and everyone poured off the coach to their waiting parents, Clare told me to wait. I remember Regan said she'd meet me outside the bus.

'Alex,' Clare said. 'This is serious. I don't know if you have a future at this club anymore. You have the wrong attitude and will not get far at all. I'm going to think about what we will do, but I will have to speak to Vic and see if that's the end for you.'

Vic Akers, the big boss, was like a god in my eyes. Clare's words shattered my world. What chance did I have at life without football?

'Alex,' I heard Regan calling from the front seat of her dad's car. 'You coming with us?'

'No, I'm going to head home,' I said, working to hold back tears.

That afternoon I got on the 277 bus home and sat at the back with my Walkman, tears rolling down my face. 'What do I do?' I thought. I had no idea how to talk about it with Mum; we never have, and still don't, broach the real raw stuff. Instead I locked myself away in my bedroom for a few days, distraught and waiting to be kicked off the team. Normally I'd write poems to get out how I was feeling, books and books of them. I loved scribbling down little verses; it was a way for me to get all my emotions out and express myself. Looking back, it was obviously my release, but I didn't realise it at the time. Writing poems was not cool, especially as I was supposed to be this tough, strong footballer. So I decided to write a letter to Clare Wheatley, to tell her how much Arsenal meant to me, please don't kick me off the team and I promise to pay you back with all my hard work – yours sincerely, Alex.

The letter worked. Clare was shocked by the strength of my plea, accepted my apology and let me stay on the team. We laugh about the situation to this day; she always says something along the lines of 'See that kid who had an attitude problem, look at her now, ay?' I always smile and say, 'yeah'. But maybe this will give Clare some more insight into that time. It wasn't an attitude problem. I was a kid that needed to be shown a bit more love and handled in a different way.

I heard about this thing called 'labelling theory' recently, which basically means how you label someone will have an influence on their behaviour and how they view themselves. For example, you might have kids who love education, love to learn, but don't take to the school system because it doesn't suit their way of learning – which was me growing up. These kids will struggle at school and probably get bad grades, and without the right support they'll be labelled a troublemaker or a dropout – even by themselves. They'll think, 'Oh, I must be a troublemaker because my teachers say so,' or 'I will live my life not achieving anything because I can't get higher than an E in my exams.' And people around them reinforce those perceptions. It's how I felt the Arsenal coaches often viewed me. Lots of kids from inner-city environments are seen as troublesome and having an 'attitude problem'. In actual fact, if people would just spend a little more time getting to know those children, getting beneath their defences, they would see the magic and that kid would have a special bond with them for the rest of their life. That kid will know you managed to see through the hard shell and the survival mechanism – and they will pay you back one way or another.

Feeling permanently indebted is a bit of a problem for me. I'm so grateful to anyone who's taken what I see as a 'chance' on me, that I feel like I always have to pay them back. My loyalty has led me into many situations where I don't get the deal I should have, or am overlooked because I'm seen as a safe bet – 'Oh, it's Alex, we know she's not going anywhere because she loves this place.' This has been a hard lesson – to not feel like you owe someone so much that you undersell yourself. It's also meant on occasion that I've been massively underpaid, although Mum's always said that as long as my car can get me from A to B and I can pay my bills, anything else is a bonus. Yet seeing the debt man work his way down our street every Thursday, knocking on doors to collect the money owed, is an image that still motivates me. It was such an evil cycle: people would take out mini-loans, then have to pay back three or four times the original amount borrowed because of the interest. When you need instant cash to pay the bills or feed your kids, you're not thinking about that, though. The lenders would then persuade you to take out another mini-loan, and it was just this dark spiral. Some weeks, we'd have to switch off all the lights and pretend we weren't home, in the hope it would give Mum another week's grace to try and scrape together some money. Most weeks, however, we'd invite the debt man in and make him tea while he filled out paperwork and counted the cash we were about to borrow. He seemed deceptively kind. I would always look at him, how nice he appeared, at the same time thinking: 'I never want a debt man knocking at my door.'

While the debt man was knocking at home, Vic Akers was starting to show more and more interest in me. Gradually, I was invited to first team training with the senior adult women, and began playing more matches with the reserves. This was a huge jump; it meant I was training with older players and was around stars like Marieanne Spacey, who was one of the biggest names in the women's game at the time. I was always too scared to really talk, but people treated me well. Reserve players like Jenny Canty and Kelly Few would give me lifts home, as training with the first team on Tuesday and Thursday nights didn't finish until 10pm, which meant I'd miss the last bus home. Jenny would always be singing on our car rides. I loved being around the strong personalities in the first teams, but training was tough and would leave me shattered. I adored it, though – it was like being back in the football cage of my childhood, having to fight and show my worth as a player. Yet despite the effort I put in, I always felt like Vic didn't take a shine to me personally. He wouldn't talk to me the way he would others; I was lucky if he said anything at all. He was often scornful or seemed to want to knock me down a few pegs.

The next step in my footballing career would be to go to Arsenal Academy but I needed a minimum of four A–C grades at GCSE to be eligible. Being at the Academy didn't mean you were on lock to play for the club – it was a way of developing young talent over two years, while giving existing players, like Regan and me, a chance to be coached every day. You lived in dormitories at the Academy, which was based in Hertfordshire. To the surprise of everyone, including myself, I managed to get five A-C grades at GCSE and could attend with the rest of the group. I knew I'd always loved being educated – I just had to do it in an entirely different way.

From the ages of sixteen to eighteen, the Academy became my primary home, Monday to Friday. In the morning I would study for a BTEC in Sports Science, with training every afternoon, and further training with the reserves and first team twice a week, if Vic willed it. At the weekend, I'd head home to Mum, who'd send me back to the Academy on a Sunday night armed with loads of packets of custard creams, my favourite biscuits. They were her way of saying, 'I can't give you much, but this is my love in the form of your favourite comfort food.' I loved it.

We didn't really have hugs and kisses in our family, because of what my dad had drilled into us. But through those custard creams, I knew I had all the love I would ever need from Mum.

Someone once asked me what my favourite biscuit was.

'Oh, I love a custard cream,' I replied, smiling.

They burst out laughing and said custard creams were a 'poor man's working biscuit'. It's not what they expected me to say.

'Why, out of all the biscuits, would you choose that?' they asked, still laughing.

This is why: that 'poor man's working biscuit' is one of graft and hard work and love. It'll remind me of Mum and home, always.

4

Strength Is . . .
Choosing To Break Away

The first time I played for England was for the U16s. Even when it's for the youth teams, there is this magical feeling about pulling on the England shirt and going out to sing the national anthem. You know you're in an elite group of people and the honour of it all really hits home. After the U16s, I got a call up for the U19s too, which at that time was the last step before the senior England team. Mo Marley, a former Everton and England player herself, had been England U19s manager since Hope Powell had stepped up as head coach of the senior women in 1998. Hope really wanted to push for more women coaches to come through, and encouraged Mo to develop the next wave of female international talent, which she did.

Speak to England players and I bet most of them would have a story to tell you about Mo and her pivotal role in their careers. Mo had confidence in me, so I loved working with her. Under her, it was the first time an England women's youth squad had made it to the European finals, and because we did well in that we qualified and then went on to the first U19s World Cup that was held in Canada in 2002. We were doing well in the tournament and had reached the quarter-final, to be played against the home nation in Edmonton. Hope Powell had flown over to be with us and to scout any players she could potentially develop into the senior side. The match against Canada was a big challenge; it was the first time most of us had played in front of a huge crowd, the size of which we'd only dreamed of – and they weren't cheering for us.

Still, there were occasions for laughs. Before travelling for the game, we had a team meeting and were instructed by Hope and the other coaches not to be distracted by, or talk to, the other teams we'd be sharing our hotel with. When we arrived at the hotel, we spotted the Brazilian team, along with their star player, a woman named Marta, who had been setting the tournament alight. No one had seen anything like her skill level in women's football and we were a bit starstruck to see her in front of us at the hotel. But remembering the rules, we didn't get distracted. As we were waiting to be allocated our rooms, I felt a tap on my shoulder and looked round to see my teammate, Fara Williams, laughing.

'Al, can you bloody believe it?' she said. 'Look at Hope over there, asking Marta for a photo.'

I started to giggle: here was our national team coach, who'd told us not to speak to other teams and players, asking for a photo with Marta in front of us all.

Dawn Scott, our physical performance manager, had

been warning us about the heat we would face in the quarter-final game and she wasn't wrong. Warming up, we were so embarrassed as a team because Dawn made us wear ugly baseball caps just to try and create some shade. Imagine! Despite Dawn's best efforts though, we struggled on the pitch and our fitness levels were nowhere near what they needed to be. Ahead of the game, we'd done so many tactical sessions about how we were going to mark Christine Sinclair, the golden girl of Canadian football. But when it came down to it, we lost the match 6-2 and Sinclair scored a hat-trick. The crowd was incredibly hostile; I remember one fan shouting at me, 'Go home, England, go home!' when I went to take a throw-in. They got their wish – we were on our way back the next day.

Sitting on the pitch after such a heavy battering, we were distraught. Mo and Hope were jogging around, patting us on the back and trying to get us to regroup. I looked up at Leanne Champ, who was one of the team's characters and a personality I loved to be around. Utterly carefree, she was. As I watched her, she burst out laughing.

'What you laughing at?' I asked.

'Reens,' she replied with her cockney-esque accent (Leanne always called me 'Reens' because she couldn't believe my middle name was Virina), 'my player scored a hat-trick. My fucking player, who I was marking, scored a fucking hat-trick. How bad is that?'

It got us all laughing. But truth be told, in football it's

never about one player. It certainly wasn't Leanne's fault. We had just witnessed the start of an incredible career: Christine Sinclair was about to stamp her name in the history books of the women's game and become a legend for her national team.

A lot of us were also about to graduate from the youth game. After that tournament, U19s life was over. I had a meeting with Mo and will never forget her words as she praised me as a player and a person.

'Alex,' she said, 'I have no doubt in my mind that you will go on and play for England. Not only that, you will captain your country. That's how much I believe in you.'

Mo had a real connection with kids. In Everton, where she lived, she was used to working with children from the streets or broken homes. Often Mo and her husband would open up their home for kids to stay in. She was one of those coaches that really got me, and knew that beneath the hard exterior, I was craving some love.

I looked up at her, almost too shy to make eye contact, and said: 'Really? Do you really believe that, Mo?'

'YES, I do, Al,' she replied in her strong Scouse accent.

I gave her a hug and thanked her for everything she had done for me and my teammates, leaving that meeting buzzing as I'd never heard anything like that sort of praise from any of my Arsenal coaches, ever. In fact, it was just the opposite. I had started to see teammates I'd played with in the U19s get selected for senior England training camps. It hurt to see those players progressing while I was left behind. It was never a jealousy thing – those were my friends and teammates. Instead, it was hurt, at the realisation that of course I wouldn't be selected for the senior England team, when all the playing time I was being given at Arsenal was five minutes as a sub for the first team here and there, or the odd ninety-minute reserve game.

Hope Powell had told the FA that just like the men's game, women also needed an U21s development team as it was a big step up for some players from U19s to senior level. By not having that U21s squad, you can lose quality players. I was thrilled to hear about the U21s team; I knew I would be a player that could compete at that level and show Hope I should be part of the senior team. But when the time came for selection for the England U21 team camps, I was overlooked. Perplexed and hurt, I sought out Dawn Scott, who I had developed a bond with after working with her at all England youth levels. I wanted honesty and knew Dawn would be frank.

'How do I get picked?' I asked her, confused. 'What do I have to do?'

Dawn told me a home truth: 'Alex, you're just not fit enough.'

I couldn't understand it. I'd played the full ninety minutes in most of my games for the England U19s and never once got subbed for my fitness levels.

Dawn explained to me that while my natural strength had seen me through at youth level, to step up would take more. The conversation felt like a body blow – but it also gave me a kick up the arse. If I seriously wanted to progress, I'd have to spend all summer focusing on my fitness with an 'I will show you all' attitude. I had a holiday to Cyprus planned for the following week, and instead of relaxing, I spent every morning running miles and doing hill sprints in the blazing sun. My mentality perhaps wasn't the healthiest – I distinctly remember feeling like the entire world was against me – but it was all I could think of doing while I was away, to drag myself to that next level. Our hotel was in the middle of nowhere in Cyprus, nothing like the places you see Premier League footballers getting some pre-season work in, at a fancy villa, equipped with a nice gym and grass fields for training. My hill sprints were done on concrete at the side of the road. It was all I had and I was not about to make excuses – or give anyone a reason not to pick me anymore.

After that summer, I was the fittest I'd ever been. I could feel my body transforming. I could run for miles and miles at a pace and not get tired. Training in Cyprus also meant the sun didn't bother me. The England U21s had to have me – they couldn't leave me out; I'd become that player who married technical skill with the ability to play back-to-back games, tournament style, with fatigue at a minimum. Not many players were at that level. I got the call that I'd made the U21s squad . . . It felt so good to have worked my way into the U21s off my own bat. I got a huge buzz from being that fit; it became a bit of an obsession. I knew that to keep playing I had to remain one of the fittest team members, or get even more so. It was the key to keeping my place.

However, this wasn't the case at Arsenal. It was during this period that I really began to understand my relationship with Vic and my role there. I loved the club and would do anything asked of me, but it always seemed that new players coming in would get called up ahead of me to make up numbers on pre-season trips or first team training. I couldn't understand it; I was more hurt by the fact that these players, who Vic was showing what I considered 'love' to, wouldn't reciprocate the investment. Within a year they would have left and be on to the next club. Yet I stayed. All I wanted was to please Vic. In retrospect, he'd clearly become a father figure to me; the first man I'd encountered with a powerful influence over my life since my dad. And just like with my dad, I never felt that love back.

Aside from my personal relationship with Vic, to this day I don't think he's given enough credit for what he's done for women's football in this country. Vic raised the standards of the women's game way before anyone else, pushing for Arsenal Ladies to be semi-professional. He lobbied to get us hand-me-down kit from the men's first team; he managed to get the men's team sponsors to give them extra boots so he could hand out their old ones to the girls (he once gave me Marc Overmars' boots – I couldn't believe it! To me, they were far too precious to wear), and he instilled in us a winning mentality and professional standards on and off the pitch. Year after year,

Vic knocked on doors at Arsenal drumming up more support and backing that allowed Arsenal Ladies to keep our name at the top of the league. The way he ran the club gave me the ethos of hard work that has stayed with me my whole life. And ultimately, my relationship with him helped me take the steps to recognise and break entrenched patterns from my childhood.

After I left the Academy at eighteen, Vic allowed me to work days in the Arsenal laundry, which was one of the jobs he'd created that allowed some players to get a working salary. By being able to offer jobs within the club, Vic managed to get international players to join – we had a strong contingent of Irish players at this time. Women players were the only ones not getting a proper pay cheque for our footballing. Wages back then weren't as staggering as they are now, but players like Martin Keown have since said they were earning at least £10,000 a week during this period. Meanwhile, on the women's side you had players like Faye White and Ciara Grant working in the Arsenal office full time, training in the evening and playing on the weekend for a yearly salary of maybe £15,000. Because I was so awkward with conversations around money, I didn't even know what a day rate in the laundry was, and I was never going to ask. Vic would call the three of us working in the laundry into his office separately, and pay us cash in hand. Can you imagine Thierry Henry doing that? There would be uproar.

At the laundry, I'd earn between £50 and £100 a week.

I was happy so long as Vic kept counting out £20 notes in front of me – I had this feeling of independence. Mum didn't need to worry about me or funding my football. I was scraping by. I'd already been working there on and off for the previous two years, so I didn't view it as anything more than an easy job, and I got to hang out with some of my teammates who also worked there. Plus, I was at the men's training ground – which not only meant being able to learn more football-wise, by being immersed in an environment where everything was about the game 24/7, but they also fed me the best lunches I'd ever had in my life. It was a win-win for me. I got food, full-on football and a little bit of cash at the end of the week.

At first I could brush off scrubbing the men's dirty kit every day. But I began to struggle more mentally when I was working at the laundry five days a week. I don't know which was worse: washing the kit on a hot summer's day when they'd all been sweating buckets, or after they'd had a muddy game in winter, when we'd be stuck over the sink desperately trying to get the dirt out of white shorts. I was also starting to see (or at least I thought I saw) that Vic had no hope for me on the pitch. Plus, just like with my dad, I always had a fear when it came to Vic. I was too shy to speak to him or knock on his door. And when he did talk to me, it was always in a slightly needling 'jokey' way that would dent my confidence (not that he knew).

Every Sunday that passed with me sitting on the

Arsenal bench, making up the numbers, Maggsy and the goalkeeper Emma Byrne would encourage me to speak to Vic and tell him it wasn't fair – but I couldn't bring myself to. All my old patterns of freezing up and remaining silent were rearing their heads.

It all came to a head in the 2004 season. Our strikers were injured and instead of Vic showing faith in me, he brought in a Scottish player who went straight into the starting line-up ahead of me. She wouldn't even train with us as a team and had to be flown in every weekend from Scotland. Yet here she was, playing, when I was stuck on the bench, disheartened and asking myself 'What am I doing?' I began to question where my life was going. Was this it? Was I always going to feel this sad? I was too scared to think about what my life would be like if I stopped playing football altogether.

The final straw was the 2004 FA Cup Final at Queens Park Rangers' Loftus Road Stadium. We were up against Charlton Athletic and won thanks to a hat-trick scored by fit-again Julie Fleeting. With one minute to go, I was surprised when Vic turned to me and told me to quickly strip off my warm-up gear and get on the pitch. I looked at him confused – he'd kept me firmly benched, so why would he choose now to put me on the field of play, with only sixty seconds on the clock? It had poured with rain all day and I was like a drowned, cold rat on the bench. Vic didn't even give me time to do a few runs and warm up, despite the risk that any player who is cold and about to sprint could potentially injure themselves – the muscles aren't ready for that level of action. I began to feel he didn't care about me at all. It wasn't anything to do with me – it was all about Fleets. He wanted the whole stadium to give her a round of applause and a standing ovation as she came off, something he told me as I was going on. I felt at that moment, he wouldn't have treated any other player like that. He wouldn't have dared. But of course, he thought I wouldn't say anything. I ran on to the pitch with tears burning in my eyes, realising that this was how Vic saw me. Or rather, he didn't see me at all.

It was the final push I needed. I knew I had to walk away from this particular family and the safety net I had relied on since I was eight. It had allowed me to escape at first, but now, like my childhood, I was being boxed in once more. I knew I had more to offer than the Arsenal coaches thought. Other teams had been sniffing around me for a couple of seasons, but I'd always turned their advances down because I was convinced that one day I'd be playing in Arsenal's first team. Now, though, my ears and eyes were open.

Marcus Bignot, the Birmingham City Ladies' boss, was the first one to really get through to me. He told me that working with him would get me loving football again, and that I needed to be at Birmingham. That was it, my mind was made up. I was off – I didn't want to feel so down and depressed all the time. There was just one thing left to do: knock on Vic's door and tell him I was leaving. It took everything I had.

Before I even started to talk, hot tears were leaking out of my eyes. I was heartbroken. Vic's office was a small one, and as he sat at his desk, looking at me, there was nowhere to escape. I stood there, waiting for him to offer me the seat opposite him, but he never did. So I just stayed there, standing, eyes on the floor.

'What's going on?' Vic said.

After what felt like an eternity, I choked out the words.

'I'm leaving,' I said. 'I have to go.'

Vic seemed unsurprised.

'I think it's for the best,' he said. 'I can't offer you playing time here as a striker. I just don't see you being the level we need.'

Why hadn't he told me this sooner? Why instead had he constantly felt the need to make me feel small? The tears continued to flow.

'I know you're an Arsenal girl, Al, but I wish you all the best.'

And just like that, my Arsenal dream was over. It had taken being more vulnerable than I ever had before and confronting Vic, not with my head held high, but in floods of tears. Going to Birmingham was a first step – it showed me I *could* strike out on my own, away from an environment that didn't seem to value me in the way I needed at that time. I'd done it – I'd chosen myself.

5
Strength Is . . .
Taking Chances

When I joined Birmingham City Ladies in 2005, I got lucky. My contract was already signed when it was announced the women's team was going to get backing from the men's side that would allow them to put more finances into the club. Marcus Bignot was more like Marcus Bigkid, talking about all the players he was going to sign over the summer.

'Just you watch, Als, we're going big,' he would say. 'We're going to challenge for trophies.'

Marcus had this infectious energy about him. He could persuade you the sun was shining, even if you knew it was raining. He would just be so loud and enthusiastic about things, you'd end up going along with whatever he said. However, he wasn't overegging his ambitions for the club. Before I knew it, Rachel Yankey and Ellen Maggs, my former Arsenal teammates, had signed with Birmingham. Along with the rest of women's football, I was totally shocked. Maggsy had been starting every game at Arsenal, was beloved and a regular fixture in the national team. But Marcus had a way about him and had sweet-talked her and Rachel into joining the revolution at Birmingham. Amanda Barr, an England striker at the time, also signed, along with Jo Fletcher, who was challenging for the number one spot as goalkeeper in the England squad. It seemed like Birmingham really had got the financial backing to sign and attract top talent.

My move was not money-motivated, though; I hadn't 'proved' anything yet, so my wages were roughly the same as I'd been making at Arsenal. I was breaking even by the time I paid for petrol or bought a return ticket from Euston to Birmingham. But so long as I wasn't having to borrow money then I felt OK.

I remember rocking up for the first pre-season day's training at Birmingham and being so happy that my friend Maggsy was there. It made everything that much easier and calmer. I was still heartbroken not to be an Arsenal girl anymore, and had begun to doubt whether I was actually any good. Maybe Vic was right, maybe I was only decent enough to be a bit-part player. At the same time, I pledged to work hard, as a thank you to Marcus for seeing something in me and giving me an opportunity to start afresh. I needed to prove Vic wrong and Marcus right – a whole new load of pressure on myself.

Football wasn't my only concern at the time, though. Dad wasn't the lone drinker in my family. My mum's side could go at it pretty heavily, too. I remember my first holiday abroad, heading to Turkey when I was thirteen with that side of the family – there were about twenty of us at the resort – the absolute best time you could imagine. But looking back, the whole holiday was based around drink. At the centre was my mum's brother, my Uncle Mickey, the life and soul of any party. He had this amazingly infectious personality. He was also drunk, all day, every day, because he was an alcoholic.

Uncle Mickey had this energy about him. He was quick as a whip and a real joker, but he paired this with a softer side. There was no mistaking the love he had for the people around him, especially for his beloved only daughter Kelly – my cousin. The bond Kelly and Mickey had was the dad-daughter relationship I longed for. He adored her. And Mickey loved the fact I played football; he was a huge Newcastle United fan and would chew your ear off with all things Magpies. He wouldn't miss a game.

He also couldn't beat his fight with alcoholism. It's not like he didn't want to quit; he knew he had to because everyone around him loved him and wanted him to be healthy. And for my cousin Kelly too, so she could grow up with her dad around. I remember one time, it almost stuck. I was fifteen. Mum told me that Uncle Mickey had finally been able to stop drinking, and he was coming down to visit us in London. The memory of Mickey walking through our front door that day is so clear. He looked like a new man, so healthy, and there was this glow about him. On the outside, he still seemed the same, cracking jokes, that sharp sense of humour still up and running, but I wondered if Mum could see what I could. In Mickey's eyes, there was a deep sadness.

For about three years, Mickey had been on the wagon. He'd fallen off for a bit, after drinking a Guinness at his partner's birthday party. When questioned at the time, he'd given a pre-planned answer – that the doctor said he'd been doing so well, the Guinness wouldn't do any harm. Obviously we knew that wasn't true but there's only so much you can say to an alcoholic. After that incident, Mickey did manage to stay off the drink for another two years, but now his health was starting to give him problems – he had tablets to take, to help with the damage the years of drinking had done to his organs.

During a visit to London with us, it became obvious that Mickey was done with sobriety. At one point, he disappeared for hours, after telling us he was going to the shop. Mum and my other uncle, Eddie, were really worried something had happened and went out searching for him. They eventually located him at the bar of the Aberfeldy Tavern, several pints down. It was another one of Mickey's relapses that highlighted once more how hard battling with alcoholism really is. Uncle Eddie wanted Mickey to move to London and live with him, so he could provide a support system for him. But Mickey's life was in Newcastle, so he headed back. A couple of months after his return, Mum and Uncle Eddie got a call from Kelly. Uncle Mickey was in intensive care, after haemorrhaging. He'd been told repeatedly by doctors what would happen if he continued to drink, and now, as predicted, his organs were finally giving up.

Being as proud as he was, Mickey had initially refused to call an ambulance, taking himself to the hospital via cab, and checking in. It was the doctors who'd called Kelly to let her know where her dad was – and that he was in a bad way. I got a call from my mum. From the moment she started talking, I could tell something was wrong.

'It's Uncle Mickey,' she said, trying to sound strong, like she always does. 'I don't think he's going to pull through this time. His liver's given up.'

Mum never said outright that he was dying. But we knew. So I asked an England teammate who lived not far from Newcastle if she could drive me to see my Uncle Mickey one last time. She said yes without any hesitation. I'll never get the image of Mickey's last days out of my head. (Cousin Kelly, if you're reading – skip this part.) When I saw him in the hospital bed, my Uncle Mickey – the man who would talk to me about my footballing career for hours and with so much pride, the man who always had a smile on his face – was gone. What confronted me was a shell of a body, shrunken to the point it almost appeared childlike. He was all bone, except for his stomach, which was swollen like a balloon. Mickey's skin was this funny shade of off-yellow because of the jaundice from the liver failure. The thought that guiltily flashed into my mind was that he looked like an Oompa-Loompa. But it wasn't funny – just devastating.

If you've never seen what jaundice looks like in real life, google it.

I've never discussed what it was like seeing Mickey that day. Not even with my mum. That's a theme, to be honest. I didn't know *how* to talk to her about it. She'd lost her brother to drink and had spent over ten years living with a man whose drinking had seen her and her children go through hell. Where do you even start with broaching that?

I didn't try to process it on my own either. The next day, I was back in Birmingham at football training, with none of my teammates or coaching staff any the wiser that I had just said goodbye to my beloved uncle. Once I walked into the dressing room, I left all my sadness and pain at the door. Football was the space I used to escape from my emotions, to tamp things down. But I didn't realise they would be waiting for me when the final whistle went, or that I was bottling up grief that would take years to explode out of me. I just thought I was getting on with things, the way my family always had. But in the back of my mind, I was waiting for the call, the one to say that Mickey had slipped away. I was so distracted, I almost couldn't focus when Marcus pulled me aside for a chat ahead of a big game we had scheduled for Sunday.

'Listen, Als,' he started. 'You're going to think I'm mad, but trust me, OK? I want you to play right back on Sunday.'

This, for non-footballing heads, was a big deal. So far at Birmingham I'd been playing in midfield, not because

I was a baller and had amazing tekkers, but because I was one of the fittest and could be that workhorse for the team. Seeing my slightly hesitant expression, Marcus ploughed on with his pitch.

'I know you haven't played there, but you played wing-back a couple of times at Arsenal so just trust yourself. I want you to get up and down the flank as much as you can.' He flashed me a smile. 'Go do it.'

I had no reason not to trust Marcus. As a coach, he'd pulled me out of what, for me, felt like a toxic environment that had festered at Arsenal and had helped me learn to love playing again. So, come Sunday, I played my first game at right back, running up and down for ninety minutes, trying to repay Marcus's faith in me (like I did every game that season). He was pleased with my performance.

What Marcus hadn't told me was that Hope, manager of the senior England women's team, was sitting in the stands that day. The next day my phone rang. It was Marcus, his voice crackling down the line with excitement.

'Als,' he said, 'you've been called into the England team. The senior England team.'

I'd already played for England at every age group from U16s to U21s. But the way my footballing career was going, I hadn't thought that a senior team call-up was on the cards. I'd left Arsenal feeling like I wasn't good enough anymore. When you are told something repeatedly, you eventually start believing it. But BAM! Here I was, with an England call-up. Even if I was just going to make up numbers and fill in for an injured Kirsty Pealling – the starting England right back – I didn't care. It felt amazing.

The next phone call I got dampened my spirits, though. Mum was on the other end, telling me Mickey had just passed away. The funeral would be in two weeks' time – the same day I was due to fly to Holland with the England team for my first game. I couldn't bring myself to tell Mum my news right then and there. As we hung up, I felt like I'd been bludgeoned by loss.

As the initial shock of Mickey's death wore off, I began to think about how on earth I was going to tell Marcus and Hope Powell that I couldn't play. I felt like I was letting not just them but Mickey down too – he'd always been so proud of my football career. Eventually I called Mum back and, in the same breath, told her I'd been called up for England and that I wouldn't be accepting, that I wanted to be by her side at Mickey's funeral.

I heard her swallow back tears before she replied, 'Absolutely not!'

'What do you mean, Mum?' I asked.

'You know Mickey loved you playing football!' she said. 'He would have none of it – he'd want you to play for England. He would not have you miss that for him.'

She took a breath and carried on.

'You're telling me that you got your first call-up the day he passed? Alex, this is meant to be. He will be there with you, you're not to be there with him. It's what he would have wanted.'

And just like that, my mum (and Mickey) made the biggest decision for me. It changed the course of my life. At half-time, we were 0-0 against the Netherlands. I was still on the bench. We were sitting in the changing room, listening to Hope give her analysis of the game so far and what the team needed to do more of in the second half. I was tucked away in a corner, not wanting to get in anyone's way. Hope finished her talk and then announced she was making a substitution.

'Alex, get ready, you're going on,' she said, then walked off. Well, my face must have been a picture. I was dumbstruck. I hadn't thought for one second I would have any game time during the whole trip, and the two scheduled matches we were there to play.

'Don't look so surprised, get your shin pads on,' called assistant coach Brent Hills, with a smile on his face. I played the second half of that game as a right back. I know my uncle Mickey was there, cheering me on, and that first England cap has always been dedicated to him. Not many people know that story. Actually, almost no one does. None of my teammates, the England manager or the staff knew that it was my uncle's funeral that day, nor the emotions that were swirling inside of me.

I think that this is where I should also mention that I don't actually have my first ever England shirt, the one I made my debut in. I knew straight away what I had to do with it, and it was to sign it and give it to Mo Marley – the first football coach in my life who believed in me and told me I would go on to be a captain and play for the England senior team. Giving her that shirt was my way of saying thank you, and those words at that time meant more to me than she ever could have known.

That first cap changed everything in my football career. I became the England starting right back when, months earlier, I'd thought I wasn't good enough to go near the national training camps. What if Mum hadn't made that decision? What if Mickey hadn't loved football?

My family taught me so much about taking chances when they're offered, even under difficult circumstances. It's advice I quickly discovered I'd have to put into practice sooner rather than later.

6

Strength Is . . .
Keeping Your Eye On The Ball

My first season at Birmingham had been incredible. I was so grateful to our manager Marcus for giving me the chance to play for ninety minutes, week in, week out. If it wasn't for that period, my footballing journey could have been very different. The Birmingham team was now filled with senior England internationals: Ellen Maggs, Rachel Yankey, Amanda Barr, Jo Fletcher, Karen Carney, Jo Potter, Emily Westwood, Eniola Aluko, Laura Bassett and myself. It should have been an opportunity for the club to push forward, not take a step back. But apparently the newly secured funding had been pulled already, which was a shock to hear. Some weeknights we were turning up, not knowing if we had a pitch to train on; you could even catch us having to run drills in the local park sometimes. Conditions were nowhere near the level they should have been, and towards the end of the season this was causing intense stress for chairman Steve Shipway and Marcus.

There was talk that it had been Karren Brady's decision to withdraw the funding, which shocked us. Surely as a woman in football, she'd be the one fighting tooth and nail for our squad? Having spoken with Karren since – and with full admiration for the woman she is – her job was to turn Birmingham City into a profitable team. Which, at a young age, she did. I've listened to a number of interviews with her where she details tough decisions that are made in business and speaks about having to remove emotion when doing so. That's what it comes down to. I would love football to be different but it's a business at the end of the day. As a player you just want it to be an amazing love story with a happy ending, but the reality is that that only happens for a small percentage of us.

Everyone in women's football had heard about Birmingham's financial problems – including Vic Akers. And Vic wasn't silly. He knew he could snap up the young talent Marcus had courted to build a new team at Arsenal, to take the club to the level he wanted: the Champions League. It wasn't long before I received a call.

'Alex, I think you should come home,' Vic said. 'You are an Arsenal girl and this is where you belong.'

Of course, I was jumping for joy. It felt like I'd finally managed to achieve what I'd been trying to for so long: for Vic to show me some love as a footballer. There weren't any feelings of resentment. To be returning to Arsenal as a 'wanted' player was everything. Five of us left Birmingham that season. There were a number of reasons for this, including late wages, but for me, I simply wanted to be back home.

And suddenly, there I was, a player in a brand-new Arsenal senior squad, getting my ninety minutes a week. Both my mindset and fitness levels were sharpening every day. Mindset and fitness go hand in hand and are everything in elite sport. When I made my senior England team debut, fitness went from being my weakness to my superpower; I could keep up my starting pace for the full ninety minutes. I'd had to push myself past my limits to achieve it, but opponents now knew they couldn't outrun me – it was a battle I'd already won – so they had to come up with something else.

Fitness also meant I could be more versatile in games, and England coach Hope Powell would play me in different positions, depending on our opposition. I remember laughing with Jill Scott in 2007; we'd just lost to the USA in the World Cup quarter-finals but we were riding high regardless – it had been the first World Cup appearance for the women's national team in nearly thirteen years. And even though we'd been beaten, we knew that we'd massively exceeded expectations to reach the quarters, which was another argument in our favour in our demand for more recognition and central contracts from the FA back home.

But that was to come. In the moment after the final whistle blew, Jill turned to me, looking for a laugh after defeat. 'Fucking hell, Alex,' she said. 'You played every position apart from goalkeeper that game!'

She was almost right; I'd started the match as right back, then switched to number seven, before finishing the game as number nine. The reason for this was that not many players were able to do four games back-to-back at the intensity needed, whereas I was a little energiser bunny. So Hope would rejig the team so I could do extra running and put pressure on opponents. Whatever Hope told me to do, I'd jump on it. I respected that woman so much. I've been lucky enough to play under some amazing managers but Hope pushed women's football forward in a way that can never be forgotten. The number of meetings and analysis sessions we went through, the double training sessions at the England camps when everyone was tired . . . Hope would drill patterns of play into us so that by the time we were allowed to trudge off to bed, we would go to sleep with visions of playing formations drifting through our heads.

Hope was adamant that we had to learn and understand the role of every single player on the pitch. A player in Hope Powell's England team could tell you the runs number nine would be making, the next moves of numbers four and eight when they were holding a defensive shape. We had to understand all the cogs in our well-oiled machine. 'You have to be a student of the game' was one of her favourite sayings. Not every player was a fan of this approach; some saw it more as dictatorship than leadership. But in the world of elite football, to make England a competitive squad, that change in mindset was needed, and I took to it – perhaps because I was already conditioned to do what I was told without question. We went from bottom of our group in the

2005 Euros to making semi-finals and finals in international tournaments. That was a big leap in the space of ten years.

In 2007, there was only one team standing between us and qualification for the World Cup. All we needed was to draw in this last match. The only thing we couldn't do was lose. The problem was, it was France, an internationally renowned side, and for good reason. As an England team we went into that match firmly entrenched as the underdogs, a scrappy little part-time national team squad who fitted in extra running sessions at local parks. Add in the fact we were playing away from home, and there were only about fifty England fans squeezed into a corner of the arena . . . the odds were firmly stacked against us.

It doesn't take a Hollywood screenwriter to be able to predict the ending – OK, we didn't *win*, but we drew. That alone felt magical. To this day, I've not been part of another match in which every single teammate put their body on the line in such a way, running the extra miles and making tackles left, right and centre. The scenes at full time were unreal. I remember collapsing in a puddle on the floor, exhausted, trying to get it into my head that we were off to China – CHINA! The other side of the world! – to compete in the most prestigious tournament going. I had no idea how many hours that would be on a plane as I'd never travelled that distance before.

As you might imagine, the party began in the dressing room and continued until the wee hours of the morning. Partying, in the early days, was the one thing I wasn't so good at – I'm pleased to say I've honed my skills since then (I learned from the best – thanks, Rachel Brown-Finnis). But I used to be so tired from the game that I couldn't find the energy to go hard – after I'd done the fun bit of chatting to everyone's families, I just wanted to head back to my room and finish off a box set. I would be exhausted but my mind would be racing, replaying every single pass or run I had made, and wondering if I should have done something better. I wouldn't go to sleep until well into the early hours of the morning. It's the same when I do big TV shows now; the adrenaline is still there and you can't come down from it.

I loved speaking to the other players' families. In those early days, I never had enough money to fly my mum over to international games. Karen Carney's mum, Marie, showed me all the love I needed in those moments though, and we'd always speak about my mum like she was there. Marie knew how much I loved cooking, and every time we turned up to the camp, Kaz would have a stack of recipe cards that Marie had collected for me from Sainsbury's, where she worked. It was so thoughtful of her to think of me that way and meant so much to me. I would text Kaz every time I tried a new recipe and tell her to let Marie know.

If we're being real, I often found it difficult when Mum actually was there – I would be distracted from the game, worrying about whether she knew where to pick tickets up from, or which entrance to meet me by after the match. Little things, that probably were just a continuation of my usual constant, low-level fretting about her wellbeing. She was just as invested in a win as I was though, and I knew that if the game was close, she'd be constantly running to the smoking area to puff on a fag because her nerves wouldn't take it otherwise.

Anyway, there we were, off to our first World Cup. To prepare us, Hope had managed to persuade the FA to let us play in the Four Nations cup, a mini-tournament also in China, with the USA, Norway, England and the home team competing. It was a great crash course for acclimatising to the conditions we'd be experiencing during the World Cup: the food, the environment, the heat – nothing would surprise us come the main event. The Four Nations went well – it was the first time we'd played the USA and won (yes, I scored the winning goal) – but what I remember most of all was the introduction to a whole new world.

We spent that trip walking around amazed at absolutely everything. There were some culture shocks, which we handled in typical Brit fashion; I remember we basically lived off cereal because we found the food in China 'alien'. Shows how far removed we were from culture and travelling the world! One night at dinner there was this awful commotion – one girl had found a chicken head in her soup bowl and was squawking just as much as the chicken probably once had. After that incident, I'll admit I ate sugar puffs for breakfast and dinner for the remainder of the trip. They were less nutritious, but the key thing was that they didn't resemble a severed bird's head. The Americans struggled with the cuisine too. We'd go down to dinner as they were finishing up and see stacks and stacks of pizza boxes. That tournament really was an exercise in national stereotypes. Dawn Scott, our physical performance coach, wouldn't let us follow suit and get takeaway, no matter how much we begged her. We argued that the Americans were the best in the world so clearly the pizza was doing something right, but she stood firm. Later I learned that training at the intensity the Americans did meant the pizza wasn't making a dent on their form. You don't see that on the high street diet plans.

Being with the Americans was also the first time I really fangirled over someone – I couldn't believe we were staying in the same hotel as the current number one squad in the world. In particular, I was awed by Abby Wambach. She was the superstar of women's football at the time. On the rare occasion women's international footballing news trickled over to our shores, it was Abby who was front page. She was a powerhouse. Dawn knew how much I loved her and asked one of the American coaches if Abby would be all right with giving me one of her shirts from the tournament. Abby being Abby instead said she'd come and meet me personally to hand it over. Nervously I waited on the tenth floor of the hotel for her to come down in the lift, racked with shyness and excitement. It was the first time in my life I'd felt anything close to being star-struck. Don't laugh, but when

I say I was a fan of Abby Wambach, I mean to the degree that her surname was the password to my first ever Hotmail account. And now, suddenly, she was standing in front of me, passing over her shirt, telling me she thought I was a great player. Trip – and life – made!

I later went on to play against Abby many times. In my last season in the American Women's Professional Soccer league (WPS), she even tried to tempt me away from the Boston Breakers (more on that later) to go and play for a new franchise she was directing. Life's funny like that.

And that wasn't the end of my Abby-related dealings. In 2020, at the start of the pandemic, I met a new friend who kept going on and on about this book she was reading and how life-changing it was. I wasn't having any of it.

'Alex,' she would say, trying to persuade me to look at it, 'it's not just a life coach book, it's this amazing love story. This woman is married but her husband has been cheating on her. She's staying for the kids because that's what society tells you to do. Then she falls in love with a soccer player, a female soccer player.

'I know you played soccer, Alex [I said this was a 'new' friend, didn't I!], I think you should read the book.'

I gave in and bought it – it's called *Untamed*, by Glennon Doyle. I could not believe what I was reading. Firstly, my friend was right, it was incredible. But secondly, the woman Glennon falls in love with is none other than Abby Wambach. I couldn't believe it. It's these coincidences and little signs from the universe that truly make me love life.

But before *Untamed* and a career in America, I was twenty-one years old and playing in my first World Cup. Hope had done everything to get us ready – the only thing she couldn't prepare us for was the excitement we were brimming over with. Our pre-Cup camp was in Macau, where we stayed in a hotel that remains, to this day, the fanciest one I ever set foot in as part of the England squad. One night we went off to the opening of another hotel, the Venetian, sister of the Las Vegas hotel. Hope had given us permission to go to the casino so long as we were back by curfew. I told myself I wasn't spending more than £10; I was quids in that night as I immediately won £150. I went and cashed it straight away, terrified that I'd get drawn into throwing away a lot of money I didn't have on a roulette table. After that I was just content to walk around, looking at expensive things. Never say I'm not easily satisfied!

Strangely, Mo Farah was training at the same Macau facilities as we were. Every morning, we'd arrive and he'd already be running laps. And when we finished our two-hour session, Mo would still be going. He would always greet us with the biggest smile too. There was a strong contingent of Arsenal players in the England team at the time and Mo is a Gooner, so we ended up snapping some photos together. It's funny which memories and moments come back to you. In pre-training, Hope had organised a game for us in the scorching heat, to get us used to playing in those conditions. I'm not sure what people think of when it comes to China's climate, but let me tell you, it can get *hot*. As high as 40°C, although that's not the average. Dawn even had us training in jumpers before we went, so we could handle it. But it wasn't enough it seemed, as halfway through our friendly match Eniola Aluko plonked herself down on the field saying she couldn't run anymore because she had heat exhaustion. For the rest of the trip, Jill Scott would burst out laughing as she recalled the sight of Eni on the sideline, lying on the bench, iced flannels placed on top of her to try to cool her down.

Friendships within the team would change as time went on, and fault lines were drawn, but in that 2007 World Cup we were united, laughing and joking with each other constantly. In that same game, I remember running down the sideline and thinking, 'Where is my partner?' I called Karen 'Kaz' Carney my 'partner' because she wasn't just my roommate, we had this incredible partnership on the field, me at number two, her at number seven. Minutes passed by and I still had no idea where Kaz was, but Hope was just gesturing at me to cover, which I did.

Suddenly, aha! There she was, back on the sideline. Running up to me, panting, she said, apologetically: 'Reens . . . I had to go.'

'What do you mean you "had to go"?' I said, bemused. Needing to pee wasn't exactly a drama for a football player.

'You know,' Kaz said, looking red-faced, and not just from the punishing rays of the sun. 'I had to *go* . . . it's the heat!'

I couldn't stop laughing for the rest of the game.

It was these moments with teammates and friends that made it all so special; you just can't replicate that dynamic and everything that goes with it. Like our team mascot tradition. Every tournament we made it to, we crowned a new mascot. It was an idea cooked up by Rachel Pavlou, another person who's done so much behind the scenes for women's football and doesn't get nearly enough credit. Whenever we qualified for a tournament, she would make a big thing of announcing the chosen team mascot for that competition. In 2007, it was Yolanda the Panda. She came everywhere with us. If you watch footage of the England team during the World Cup, you can spot Yolanda, often perched on top of the dugout. Every day a different player took their turn to look after Yolanda and make sure she had a great time.

It wasn't all fun and games though. At our first match location in the Cup, the players were having the time of their lives in the hotel pool. That is, until Hope ripped into us all at a meeting later that night.

'What do you think this is?' she raged. 'A pool party? We can't even get you in the pool for recovery sessions after training, and here you are in China, playing volleyball and all sorts. I'm not having it, it's banned.'

It sounds funny now but at the time it was the worst feeling in the world to be in Hope's doghouse. Think of your most painful school telling-off and then multiply that by ten. It couldn't dim our spirits for long though; even our eventual quarter-final exit wasn't as much of a blow as it could have been. We'd set a new standard for modern women's football and every part of the journey had been a memory to keep forever.

Good and bad, these are the things that stay with me when I remember the joys that football opened me up to. Being part of what was, to this day, the best Arsenal women's team there's ever been. We were the INVINCIBLES for the course of a season and a half. We did the same run as the men's team – and for even longer: 108 games undefeated. That's one for the books.

It's difficult to articulate how we knew as a team what we were going to achieve in that 2007 season, but somehow we had this quiet confidence that in Vic Akers' twentieth anniversary year as manager of Arsenal Ladies, we were going to win the quadruple. And we did.

If I'm honest, we already knew we had the league done and dusted. No one could really match us, we were that strong. It would only be a cup final or Champions League leg that would stop us sweeping the board. Lo and behold, a spanner was placed in the works in the Champions League semis. We knew we could win against the Danish side we were facing when, all of a sudden, our star player, Kelly Smith, got red-carded and sent off. I remember the crowd really getting on Kelly's back, booing her as she walked off. Kelly, being Kelly, saw red and suddenly her middle finger went up towards the ref and all the fans, while this big smile spread across her face. Kelly had other moments like this in her career – I remember playing against Sweden in the final group game of the 2005 Euros. We were defending a corner and this Swedish player wouldn't stop moving around. I saw Kelly reach out and literally yank the girl's long braid. Then she looked at me and winked! Later she said she didn't know what went through her head in those moments, her brain would just do 'crazy shit'. Indeed.

Those of us still on the pitch started laughing in disbelief, unable to believe she'd actually just flipped her middle finger – at the ref! The giggles persisted after we won the match and had made it as the first British women's team in a Champions League final. But they stopped when Vic delivered the news that Kelly's little stunt had resulted in a two-game ban, meaning she'd miss both legs of the final. It was a real blow as Kelly was our top player.

The first leg of our Champions League final was due to take place in Sweden against Umea – the best of the best. And I would be marking Marta, the best player in the world. You'd think I'd be scared, but I couldn't wait. I'd always told Hope Powell I wanted to be the best right back in the world. At our annual January camp that year, I'd repeated my goal when Hope asked me what I wanted to achieve. She looked at me seriously and said: 'Well, you are a long way off.' That cut me deep. I hadn't said I *was* the best, just that I wanted to be. Hope didn't like people getting ahead of themselves and had a knack for shooting them down – sometimes prematurely. Or maybe it was her way to try and get you to work even harder – I don't know, but I'd been hoping for positive reinforcement and encouragement that if I worked hard, it wouldn't be a pipe dream (and it wasn't – later I would achieve it under the guidance of American coaches), but instead I got the names of the right backs Hope thought were better and was told to study them. On that list was the German right back at the time, Kerstin Stegemann, and Heather Mitts, the American golden girl. I watched both Heather and Kerstin, studying their game. They were both great one-vs-one defenders and could read the game so well. But I also remember watching Germany and thinking, 'Why would I try to be someone else? I am going to be me, Alex Scott, not an imitation of the German right back.'

I was so excited to be seeing the best of the best up close and playing against them. This was one of those things I loved, and still do: a chance to test myself. I crave a challenge. Umea were the super team of women's football. They had the money and sponsors to attract players from all over the world, including Marta, the Brazilian.

Pre-game, a few of us went to scope out the pitch. There was a car parked in the centre circle. I asked Emma Byrne and Rachel Yankey what the heck it was doing there.

'Reens, don't you know?' Emma said. 'The player of the match wins that car.'

No way! It was an incredibly fancy car. I began to imagine, what if . . .

But there wasn't much time for daydreams because we had a match to play. An incredibly tight one at that. No one expected us to even compete with this team full of stars, but we did. I'd been prepared for how quick Marta was – remember, I was the energiser bunny of the team – so my main worry was her insane amount of skill. But as a defender equipped with knowledge from the national team camp, I completely understood my role as a full back and was loving it, attacking and defending with confidence. Late into the game, only minutes on the clock to go until the final whistle, I found myself near Umea's goal. All I remember is hearing Vic's voice boom at me: 'SHOOOOOOOT!' I was that terrified I followed his instruction and booted the ball as hard I could – it flew over the goalkeeper straight into the top corner and the back of the net. I had scored the only goal of the game and handed us the first leg of the Champions League final. My teammates swarmed me to celebrate; even Emma raced up from her goal position to be part of the moment. The whistle blew. Not only had we won the game, I'd been awarded player of the match. All I could think about was that fancy car. It was mine!

'Emma, Yanks,' I said, all excited. 'How will they get my car to me?'

They looked confused.

'I won the car!' I explained. 'What happens? Do you think they'll drive it over? Is there a ferry?'

Emma and Rachel looked at each other and burst out laughing.

'Reens,' said Emma, gasping for air, 'it was a joke . . . we were joking with you!'

They never let me live that one down! Although as I write this, I'm wondering if maybe that joke did allow me to dream the 'what if . . .' and helped manifest being named player of the match. Who needs a fancy car anyway? Not many people can say they have a Champions League medal and their name etched in the Arsenal history books as the only goal scorer. You can stuff your car up your arse! But not literally. That would cause problems.

Emma liked to play tricks on me. When I was younger, I was absolutely obsessed with, and terrified of, tornadoes. I remember watching *Twister*, this 90s film with Helen Hunt and Bill Paxton barrelling round Oklahoma, chasing tornadoes, and that was it – I was frightened for life. Like lots of people do when they're scared, I studied absolutely everything I could get my hands on to do with tornadoes, including how they developed and formed, where they were most likely to hit, and so on. I knew that because of the flow of cold and hot air in England, we weren't as likely to get the same devastating wind storms that America does, but I still planned for the eventuality regardless. I worked out routes to take my mum and brother to safety; I would save all our lives. One pre-season, Vic told us the team had been invited to America – Tulsa, Oklahoma to be exact.

As exciting as this was, of course I couldn't go – that's where they have tornadoes. It's not too far from Tornado Alley. I expressed my concern to Vic in what I thought was a rational and scientifically evidenced manner. He told me I was being stupid and of course I was going.

Arriving in Oklahoma, at first all went well. I got through our first day; we trained, did a coaching camp and everything seemed fine. The next afternoon I was relaxing in my hotel room when the phone rang. I picked it up.

'Ma'am,' came an American-accented voice on the phone. 'We have tornado warnings in the area. We have to ask you to head to the basement of the hotel.'

I started gibbering. 'Are you sure?' I asked, hands shaking.

'Ma'am, this is urgent,' the woman on the other end said. 'You have to head to the hotel basement now.'

'OK, THANK YOU, I WILL HEAD THERE NOW,' I practically yelled back. I froze. My roommate, Rachel Yankey, was nowhere to be seen and I didn't want to leave her to face the tornado alone. But I had to get to the basement.

Terrified for my life, I ran into the hallway, where Emma and Yanks were just emerging from a room.

'Reens, you OK?' Emma asked, concerned.

'Girls, there are tornado warnings,' I announced, flustered. 'Did you not get a call? We have to head to the hotel basement NOW.'

They didn't seem too concerned. 'We didn't get a call, are you sure?' Yanks asked.

'Yes!' I told them. We were running out of time, and I began simultaneously pleading with them to hurry up while banging on the doors of other teammates, panicking that they too might have missed the call.

I became aware that Emma and Yanks were not treating the news with quite the same gravitas as I was. In fact they were pissing themselves laughing.

'What are you doing, guys?' I demanded crossly. 'This is serious!'

'Reens,' Emma said, choking back laughter. 'It was me, I called you to trick you!'

They fell about all over again.

Fuckers! I was so gullible. To me, this was absolutely no joke but the rest of the team were beside themselves when they heard that one and how I'd fallen for it. Days later, tornado warnings did go off in the area and I once again shat myself, only to be told they were routine fire alarms. Maybe there is such a thing as being too careful.

The year 2007 was written in the stars. It wasn't just Vic's twentieth anniversary with Arsenal Ladies, it was also his sixtieth year on this earth. As a team we clubbed together to get the gaffer a present and I decided to write a poem (as you do). At the end of our team meal to celebrate him (at a Harvester, if I remember correctly), I announced to Vic that I'd written this poem and proceeded to read it out. Thankfully, it got a big round of applause from the squad and Vic loved it so much he got it framed, saying I'd managed to encapsulate the special feeling of what it meant to be part of the anointed group for that once-in-a-lifetime season: the Invincibles.

In addition, during the 2007 World Cup, it was announced that a new professional women's league in America would be starting in 2009. Only the best of the best would be selected to play and only five international players could be drafted. I didn't think American coaches would even know my name or waste one of their five picks on a right back.

Then I got a life-changing phone call from Tony DiCicco. Tony DiCicco was the main man. He'd coached the USA team to World Cup glory at the Rose Bowl in 1999, the famous victory which saw USA defeat China on penalties with Brandi Chastain scoring the winning pen and whipping her top off to celebrate. It was an iconic moment, and the 90,000 people packed into a stadium was a record for a women's football match that was only beaten in 2022. Tony had been the steady hand behind some of the greatest players in the game's history, and had helped change the course of women's football forever. Tony was a legend – one sadly no longer with us, after passing due to cancer in 2017. Now he was calling *me*, telling me he'd been blown away with my World Cup performance and was drafting me as a third-round pick to the Boston Breakers. My road to Boston wasn't exactly smooth – more of which in the next chapter – but thankfully I ended up there and it was one of the best decisions of my life.

My departure from Arsenal was very different from the last time I had knocked on Vic's door a couple of years before. Vic knew there was not much he could really do to stop me making the move stateside even if he tried. The game in England was still part-time, and we were still only training Tuesday and Thursday evenings after everyone had left the training ground. I was juggling working part-time as a teacher now, teaching sixteen- to eighteen-year-olds at the same academy that I went to. Life can be so funny sometimes. It was one of those days when I was struggling mentally, wondering if I would be working in the Arsenal laundry for the rest of my career, when I'd got a call from someone at Oaklands College. They had seen me do a talk in Hertfordshire and seen my connection working with kids and asked me if I could come in for a chat about a position there. I thought it was a joke but it turned out to be true. I was offered a job teaching the same subjects to both Arsenal girls and Saracens rugby boys, plus a different class that was made up of kids who were not part of a sports academy but wanted to get a BTEC in sport science. Alongside this, I would work towards getting my postgraduate certificate in education, funded by Oaklands, and they would give me all the support I needed on the job. Here I was, only twenty-two myself, teaching young adults not far off my age, but I loved it. I wanted my classes to be everything opposite to the experience I had when I was at school, and it seemed like I was managing to do just that as 'word on the street' (from the other teachers) was that the kids loved coming to my class – gold star for me!

But it was hard. I remember getting on the team bus after an Arsenal game in Doncaster on a Sunday, so tired from the game, but straight away I would get on my laptop and fill in my lesson plans and mark assignments to try and get ahead for the week. I was juggling three roles: Alex Scott the Arsenal player, Alex Scott the England player, and Alex Scott the part-time teacher – all to try and earn some money to support me as I tried to be the best right back I could ever be.

So even though I was riding high off the back of my first World Cup and having won a historic quadruple with Arsenal, the opportunity to play professionally with and against the best, week in week out, was something I'd be foolish to turn down, and Vic knew that. He gave me his full blessing and said, 'When you are ready to return home, the door will always be open.'

Tony based his team dynamic around family. We danced together as a team before every game and went out as a team after every home game. Families were allowed to come to team hotels. Tony also went out of his way to encourage his players to get to know *his* family as well. My time at Boston made me reconsider a lot of the ideas we'd been taught as givens in England.

Before I joined, people kept trying to pit me against Heather Mitts, the current right back and a star of US soccer. I kept getting the same questions: 'Alex, are you making the right decision to play in the US? Suppose you don't play? How are you and Heather Mitts going to play on the same team?'

I would be lying if I said there weren't times when I let those thoughts creep in. But I would quickly snap out of it and tell myself how stupid it would be to turn down the opportunity of a lifetime to be a professional footballer in what was going to be the best league in the world, all because of a bit of healthy competition. Competition is what's needed in order to be the best in anything you choose to do.

When I got to Boston, after completing our first preseason and scrimmage ('friendlies' in the UK) games, it was clear that, actually, I was going to be the starting right back and Heather would move over and play on the left. Instead of creating an awkward atmosphere or taking this out on me, Heather showed what a classy human being she is. Besides us becoming really close friends and her helping me to adapt to life in Boston, she had me stay behind after training and at least three times a week she would help me practise kicking long balls with my left foot, because she said I was weaker on that front. I never forgot how much that meant and how hard that must have been for her because, ultimately, Heather went on to lose her place as right back in the national team and had to make the choice to leave Boston in the second season.

Another stand-out example of the difference between

the American mentality and the English one happened while we were doing pre-season training down in Miami. Americans love fitness drills. They just will not stop running. On this occasion, we were doing speed endurance runs, which is a certain number of sprints, running back and forth for three or four sets. Kristine 'Lil' Lilly, an American legend, was like a machine, leading the way. In my last set, I came in just behind her and would have jumped for joy if I hadn't been gasping for breath as I made it over the line. It felt so good it was over, but then:

'Alex, get back here!' I heard Lil shout. Instead of standing on the side, watching the rest of the team complete the drill, she was now running alongside Tiffany Weimer, who was struggling at the back and was starting to talk herself out of being able to complete the exercise. As she ran, Lil instructed me to take it in turns with her to sprint alongside Tiffany until she made it to the finish line. I found myself running in step with Tiff, shouting, 'We can do this!' The rest of the team had now finished and were cheering her on as well. Crossing the line, Tiff fell straight to the floor but it was job done, she'd completed it. I had this incredible feeling inside me, knowing I'd helped a teammate. As we were packing up for the day, Lil called me over. 'Scottie,' she said, 'you're only as strong as your weakest link. If Tiff fails that drill, we all fail. It's why we help our teammates get through certain things, it's how we stick together as a team.' I knew then and there that I was going to love playing in America and love Kristine Lilly being my captain. That's a player driving team standards right there, without a manager having to say a word.

Back in England, the environment was different. Take the 2009 Euros. It was another step forward for our national side; we reached the final and won a silver. Don't get me wrong, we got absolutely battered in our last game against Germany, who had already had a bunch of T-shirts printed reading 'Champions'. Hope held a team meeting dedicated to fuming about this move, raging that it was so arrogant of the Germans to think they had won before they had even played. At the time I agreed, but after America I wasn't so sure. The elite mindset is believing 100 per cent that you are going to win – so why not have the T-shirts made and ready to go? In England, we often have this mentality of restraint that I think actually holds a lot of people back.

Hope and some of the England staff took to calling the five of us that were playing in the WPS 'big timers', which for me wasn't funny. Whenever we'd meet for training camp, one staff member in particular would always greet us with a needling: 'Here they are, the big timers.' It had that little edge to it. I would laugh politely in response but could never be bothered to say anything. There was this underlying current that, somehow, playing in America meant we were getting too big for our boots. When in reality, being in America was making me a better player for England. But it helped me understand the part of the English character that feels it has to cut others down to size, rather than encourage them to grow.

Tony DiCicco was certainly of the latter camp. He told me that at the 2011 World Cup, the rest of the world would see I was the best right back.

'You already are,' he continued, 'but you need to believe it.'

I couldn't say anything in return but a mumbled 'thanks'. I'd never had this form of management before. It had been mostly stick and very little carrot, which got physical results, but this . . . this was positive reinforcement. I already felt like I owed Tony the world for taking a chance on me in the first place, but now I was determined: I was going to do everything I could to repay his faith in me. He thinks I'm the best? Well, I'm going to be the best. For him.

In the event, we were knocked out of the 2011 World Cup against France on penalties. Sometime after the match, there was collective hurt on the part of the team upon reading Hope had accused 'certain players' of 'cowardice' for not stepping up to take a penalty. This is where I'm such a big believer in mindset. When Hope asked the team who wanted to take a penalty, she was greeted by blank faces and no response. If the England team had been instilled with a positive mindset, then I think you would have seen a whole load of hands go up. But we were managed through fear: fear of losing, fear of doing something wrong, fear that your contract could be taken away from you with a month's notice, especially as it was – for the most part – covering each player's basic living costs. Players were scared, and in that moment

thinking 'What if I miss?' rather than 'What if I score?'.
That England team was so tightly managed, you saw
thirty-year-old women having to ask permission to go to
the local shop for a snack. Now suddenly that was flipped
and players were tasked with decision-making power at
a moment that was definitely one of the biggest in our
careers. None of my teammates were cowards. I just
think that no one – including management – had been
in such a situation before. In hindsight, it was a moment
to learn from. If only it had been managed differently.

Still, Tony's prediction proved correct. A couple of
weeks later, the 'team of the tournament' was announced
and it was official: I was regarded as the best right back
in the world. To that end, I felt like I'd repaid both Hope,
who has been such an influential figure in my life, and
Tony DiCicco for believing in me from day one, which
meant absolutely everything.

Another major 'wow' moment was the 2012 Olympics. It was a landmark event. For one, it was just round
the bloody corner from where I grew up. And it was this
cornucopia of new experiences in an area of London I
thought I knew like the back of my hand. The athletes
were let loose in the Olympic Village Food Hall – my
word! I'd never seen anything like it, not even at Chrisp
Street Market. There was just so much food from all over
the world. I found myself wandering round and round
in circles, drooling but utterly paralysed by choice, not
having a clue what I was going to eat. Being able to show
Mum around the Village was a particular highlight for

me. Her reaction to it was so *Mum* – every time she sees something of that ilk, she goes, 'Oo, this is fancy, isn't it?' It always makes me smile. I still don't know what to do with my Olympic memorabilia. I often think about giving it away, but in the end it always seems to stay where it is. I suppose it's good to have the reminder, although the memories are strong without it: like playing at Wembley. It was the first time playing at that ground for most of us, and we were playing Brazil, which meant I was up against Marta once more, requiring my best game. My confidence was given a boost by the Brazilian manager, who said he thought the way I played as a full back meant I was Brazilian and perhaps they needed to check my family history so I could play for his team. I loved that. Three years in America had really put me at the top of my game.

Seventy thousand fans turned up to cheer us on to a win at Wembley. There we were, dancing to S Club 7 telling us to 'Reach! For the stars' before stepping out in front of the biggest crowd any of us had ever witnessed. The fact we won 1-0 just went to crown the day as a special one in women's football – and showed that, if organised correctly, fans will come! Even though we got knocked out in the quarter-finals, we were still allowed to stay in our digs in the Olympic Village, which I did. There was also a daily raffle, where we could get a free ticket to an event where there were spare seats. Rocking up to disciplines I'd never watched live before was an incredible experience, especially as I got to cheer on

Team GB athletes in the same way I'd been supported. Also, I'm just putting it out there: the parties. That's all I'll say on the matter.

Perhaps the most magic moment of all was when a group of us managed to blag our way into the main stadium to watch Usain Bolt smash his 100 metres record. How we did it, I will never know. But I felt properly alive then, and just so lucky to be there. Even as people who were no strangers to making history ourselves, watching it happen in front of you was pretty trippy. A week later we were part of the official Olympics closing ceremony – but the real one came later, in the food hall, when all the athletes were lining up for McDonald's. That's how you knew the Games were done: the top-level athletes could order as many fries and chicken nuggets as they wanted.

I could go on and on with more footballing stories and the magical moments along the way . . . As for the most memorable moment in my footballing career, well, you're going to have to read a bit further on to discover what that was. All I'll say now is I learned from the Germans at the 2009 Euros and had the party planned.

Football has brought so much joy to my life, it's immeasurable. And even when I'm not on the pitch, it's still there. Where would I be without the beautiful game? Probably not writing this. It's been an honour, and will remain so. Always.

7

Strength Is . . .
Learning To Love

OK, deep breath, here goes. I'm scared to write this next chapter. I've thought a lot about how I can maybe skirt around one of the most intimate parts of my life, or leave it out completely, but the fact is, I can't. I would be lying, not just to myself but to all of you if I erased this from my story. It's a tale as old as time – about when I fell in love. First love. The proper stuff. Truly, madly, deeply.

Kelly Smith was a superstar in my world when our paths crossed – think the David Beckham of women's football, if you really want a comparison. I was eighteen years old. But at the time, I wasn't bothered about her fame. She'd gone to play in America so, in all honesty, I grew up not knowing much about her. She was a faraway legend, a talent you only heard mentioned in reverent terms or via gossip about her injuries.

But in 2005, Kelly moved back to England, nursing various physical ailments. With the Euros on the horizon, she began to train at the very camps I'd just started attending a year previously. At first, she kept herself to herself. She would train and then disappear, either to the physio's office or her hotel room, only talking to Hope Powell, the doctors or Faye White. Yet there was something about her . . . in the snatched moments we did interact, I couldn't help being cheeky around her, trying to draw a smile out of her.

This wasn't out of character; I'd always seen my role in the England squad as the person who'd try and encourage my teammates to push away the negative stuff and let loose, especially in those high-pressure moments. When I joined the senior team, it blew my mind to find that there was no music played in the changing room. Imagine! Not only is music such a stress-reliever, it's also a hugely powerful way to connect people – connect a team. Yet in the dressing room that housed England's most elite footballers, there was only silence. So I started putting my tunes on, earning a reputation as the bolshie, fresh-faced young one who lugged her big Bose speaker everywhere and always left her door open on the team hotel floor, music blaring, inviting everyone in for a chat.

But with Kelly, I felt my need to make her smile came from somewhere deeper, a stirring in the pit of my stomach. And my jokes got her grinning. I remember my teammates being shocked at my nerve at cheeking this legend, telling me in hushed whispers that 'You can't say that to Kelly!'

'Why?' I asked. I always see everyone on the same level, no matter what role they play. And there was something about Kelly Smith I just couldn't shake.

I think I was falling in love with her before I even realised that's what it was. Our actual relationship took a lot
longer to get going; the build-up was delicate, tentative
and so exciting. Pivotal moments come back to me – like
when we played our opening 2005 Euros game against
Finland, and midway through the game I had Kelly
screaming at me like I was a moron because I didn't aim
the ball her way when I took a throw-in. We won anyway
and later that night, when I was chilling in my room, I
heard a soft knock on my door and in walked Kelly. This
was a first. She never came to anyone's room. And she
certainly didn't come to anyone's room wearing the
slightly abashed look she had on her face just then.

'I wanted to say I'm sorry for yelling earlier,' she told
me. 'It was the adrenaline.'

I cut her off, laughing, telling her not to be so stupid,
even though deep down I felt a rush of warmth and
appreciation at her words, and realised in the same
moment I didn't want her to leave. So I asked her if she
wanted a cup of tea. She said yes.

Never had conversation been so easy. I'm smiling
recalling it. We talked and talked – until my roommate
Kaz came back and Kelly instantly shot up, becoming
awkward and uncomfortable.

'Thanks for the tea,' she said, and darted out the door.

Kaz looked surprised – she was used to all our
other teammates popping in for a chat. But not Kelly
Smith.

That was the start of something. Not on the

footballing side because we ended up bottom of our group. But from then on, Kelly would visit my room most days for a cup of tea and a chat. Then the tournament ended and we went our separate ways. Or so I thought. I was on my way out of Birmingham at this point, back to Arsenal – 'coming home', as Vic called it – along with my England teammates Rachel Yankey, Kaz Carney and . . . Kelly Smith.

From the off, everyone at Arsenal could see what was happening before we even had a name for it ourselves. We'd wind up sitting next to each other on the team coach all the time, laughing together, chatting during training, grabbing any chance to talk or just be around each other. I could see Kelly was not open in that way around anyone else. And I suppose, neither was I – I might outwardly have been the team cheerleader, but with Kelly the connection ran deeper than I'd ever felt before. I had no idea how to make the first move, however – I still don't to this day. Maybe it's shyness, maybe it's a fear of rejection. But finally, one day during that season, I picked up my phone to see a text from Kelly.

'Cld I take u for dinner after training?' it read.

'YES,' my heart screamed, before my brain went into panic mode, sounding the alarm. Oh my god, Kelly Smith was asking me on a DATE. Shit! I pulled it together long enough to text back and confirm.

Training that day was excruciating – I suddenly went all shy, not even able to look her in the eye, knowing that in a few hours we would be crossing a boundary that meant our relationship would never be the same again. I was terrified – and fizzing with excitement.

I don't even remember what restaurant we went to, some place in St Albans, with lots of wine to calm our nerves (or so I thought at the time). We could have been anywhere in the world – all Kelly and I were focused on was each other. A warm feeling flooded me as we talked and brushed hands; I felt like we were both lit up like firecrackers. I knew this was something I couldn't ignore. Of course, we went home together. And for the next eight years, we were in a relationship that even today still makes me smile. That doesn't mean it was easy – we both had our demons. I think hers showed themselves earlier than mine. On date two, in fact.

Kelly had planned a surprise evening for me. She knew I was mad for musical theatre (I can't resist getting lost in a story as it is, but with the added bonus of great tunes? Sign me up) and had booked tickets for *Mary Poppins*, aware of how much I loved the film. We went for drinks before the show. And drinks during the show. Then drinks after the show. Something was different. I hadn't seen this side of Kelly before; there was an arrogance and aggression to the way she was moving around, a hard edge that frightened me. At one point I told her I was going to end the night and go home, and she lost it.

'Go home then, be boring!' she drunkenly screamed at me. 'Ruin a good night!' On and on, ranting incoherently. I welled up, fleeing the bar and realising in the moment just how deeply in love with her I already was – her ability to hurt me was a gut punch. Through tears, I tried to hail a taxi, when Kelly barrelled up, contrite and begging me to go back to hers. In shock, I agreed. That car ride changed everything.

Kelly Smith, it turned out, was an alcoholic. She'd been to rehab already, she told me, but it was a disease she was still coming to terms with. Looking back, should I have run for the hills? Not because Kelly didn't need and deserve love, but because I was a nineteen-year-old who'd already lost, in different ways, a father and uncle to alcohol, had seen her childhood innocence sacrificed to the bottle. Now here I was, madly in love for the first time in my life, with an alcoholic. It didn't bode well.

I couldn't have known about Kelly's illness when I was first drawn to her. But once I did find out, I made a choice that, in the moment, was incredibly naive, but also one I will never regret. Instinctively, I could see and feel the love she had for me, the happiness that flooded through her when she was with me. It was beautiful. Maybe I could be a healing force, I thought. I could *help* her, love her and save her from this darkness. She was an amazing person, full of life, that just had this one little demon. No problem – right?

For anyone reading who is an alcoholic or loves an alcoholic, you'll know this was really misguided of me. Alcoholism is a disease. It doesn't matter how much someone loves you when you're an alcoholic. That alone isn't enough to overcome it. If it was, my Uncle Mickey would have been golden. My dad would have sailed through. And Kelly Smith would have stuck to sobriety from the minute I got into the taxi with her.

I didn't run away, of course. After that second date, our relationship only became more intense, full of excitement and laughter. The butterflies in my stomach had fully taken flight. I was spending most of my nights with Kelly, in the house she shared with Faye White. It feels strange to try and explain that at the same time as we were walking-on-air happy, I was also seeing first-hand the true extent of Kelly's battle with drink. I will never forget the certain look in her eye that gave away when she'd been drinking. Picture this: you're sitting on the sofa, talking, giggling, sort of paying attention to whatever is burbling away on the TV in the background. Really, you're focused on the person you're with, and in turn they're fully present and in the moment. Then they'll excuse themselves – 'I'm just nipping to the loo,' they'll say. It only takes five minutes, but the person who returns is completely different to the one that left – eyes blurry, suddenly struggling to string a sentence together.

I was so naive in the early days. I couldn't believe how this change could take place in the space of five minutes. Kelly hadn't even gone to the kitchen – surely I'd have seen if she was pouring herself a drink? I couldn't figure it out. I would ask, 'Kel, have you had a drink?' and she would assure me: 'No, Alex, of course not.' So at the start, I didn't push it. I'd just sit there in the knowledge that the Kelly Smith I loved so deeply, that warm, engaging, intelligent woman, had been replaced by Kelly number two. That Kelly was distant. Numb. It was a hard process for me – a lot harder than I admitted to myself at the time.

It's very difficult to write this – I almost feel like a hypocrite. There were many amazing nights we had that involved drinking – hitting the clubs in Soho, dancing till the wee hours. Kel would always get us doubles and we'd do shots; I'd often be drinking to keep up with her. But I was in love. If she was happy, I was happy.

That was off the pitch. At work, we were still keeping our relationship under wraps. We didn't want it to interfere with our football, but word began to spread, as it tends to in the close-knit world of women's football. I was so worried about this; I never wanted to be seen as 'Kelly Smith's girlfriend'. I was still up-and-coming and determined to make my name on my own terms and because of my ability; I didn't want people to think I was only getting picked to keep Kelly happy.

This is still an issue I struggle with when dating, even to this day. When I was starting to make my way in broadcasting, this very cute, very famous young guy really went out of his way to woo me. I won't reveal his name but he was in a boy band. A big one. And he was very sweetly and doggedly pursuing me. I had nothing to lose, but kept telling myself that my media career was just starting – if I got papped with this guy, I would always be known as so-and-so's girlfriend and people would think I'd only reached a certain level by riding off the back of his fame. So besides a few kisses here and there, I didn't take things any further because of that – how stupid. If you're reading this, Mr Boy Band, now you know why I really kept you at a distance. But you are a very nice, cute guy, and who knows – maybe we'll end up at the same after-party again soon . . .

But way before boy banders, there was Kelly, and the pressure I felt to hide our relationship as much as possible at work, to protect myself. Gossip spread, though, and after a couple of months Hope found out.

Until Kelly opened up about her alcoholism to the public in 2011, only a very small number of people knew about her problems. Hope was one of them. In 2004, Hope had helped bring Kelly back from the US when she was in a very dark place. She was deeply invested in helping Kelly get healthy, assisting her through rehab and then on to working with Tony Adams' Sporting Chance clinic. Away from England camps, Hope would always check in on Kel – not just as a manager, but as a friend. I remember the phone call from Hope when she discovered our relationship like it was yesterday.

I was in the room when Kel's phone started ringing.

'Kel, it's Hope,' I called. At this point, we thought Faye White, Kelly's housemate, was the only person who really knew how serious our relationship was, because she constantly had to put up with being around two people who were madly in love.

Kelly picked up the phone. 'Hi, Hope, how are you?'

she said. There was some small talk and then I heard my name mentioned.

'What, Alex Scott?' Kelly said, looking at me. She pursed her lips, then walked out of the room, the phone still pressed against her ear. Thoughts were racing through my head. Maybe Hope was telling Kelly I was being dropped from the squad, or had found out I'd been in a club in Soho when I shouldn't have been. I considered every possibility bar the conversation that was actually coming.

Kelly reappeared. 'Well, that was interesting,' she said. There was a smile on her face, but it wasn't happy.

'What happened?' I asked. 'Why did you mention my name?'

'Hope asked me if we were together,' she said. 'I told her "yes".'

Kelly went on to tell me that Hope was worried. 'Don't mess Alex up,' she had warned Kels. 'It's a lot for her to take on, Kelly, she's young.'

Hope is a wise woman, but I don't think she knew how head-over-heels we were at that stage – I'm not sure even wild horses would have pulled us apart. And as time wore on, she saw we made each other happy and that I was a good influence on Kelly.

Kelly's influence on me, however, was slightly more complicated. On the one hand, she was teaching me how to love and be vulnerable in a way I had never experienced before and, if I'm being brutally honest with myself, haven't since. That's partly because since Kel, my guard has been up, and for a long time, I haven't done the work necessary to heal from it. Even in those early stages, some of my teammates clocked that I was changing to try and help Kelly. It wasn't her fault – she never asked me to do it – I was just trying to care for her but going about it all the wrong way, which ended up exacerbating the hurt we both felt. I started going to fewer team events and parties, scared that if I went out and had a drink, Kelly might smell it on me and be triggered into drinking herself. In retrospect, this wasn't logical at all – on the occasions I did go out solo, Kelly would usually drink on her own anyway. But I was placing the burden of regulating her drinking on myself – an impossible task. This was evident when we did go out together; even though I loved to dance, I would hover by Kelly's side all night, because if I dared to venture to the dance floor, she would disappear to the bar.

Even though I had grown up surrounded by alcoholics, I didn't learn the specific tricks employed by addicts until I dated Kelly. Ordering two drinks at once and downing one before returning to our table. Stashing vodka bottles – vodka because supposedly you can't smell or taste it on someone – in her bedroom cupboard, something I discovered one day while looking for wellies. Confronted with her stash, I was so sad and angry but also, weirdly, embarrassed. I didn't even feel like I could say anything because then Kelly would think I'd been going through her belongings. I felt so alone with the secret; everyone around her thought she was managing, but she wasn't. Despite all this, there were only three periods in our eight-year relationship that we either took a break or nearly broke up. The first had been that date to see *Mary Poppins*. The second was at an awards show. A teammate told me she'd spotted Kelly embarrassing herself while drunk. Suffice to say, I was not impressed. I'd had enough. I handed my teammate the drink I was holding and told her I was going home, tapping out a text to Kelly that basically said I'd had enough and was leaving her. Instead of heading to Kelly's, I went back to my mum's.

'I didn't expect to see you here, Al,' she said, upon opening the door. 'Where's Kelly?'

I mumbled something about not fancying the after-party and Kelly wanting to stay there. Even though I hadn't officially told Mum that Kelly was my partner (and wouldn't until two years into the relationship), she knew from the start. She was even looking after Kelly's dog that evening. And when I turned up, looking shell-shocked, she knew something was wrong. I put my phone on silent and tried to ignore the multiple calls and texts coming in from Kelly. Just as I'd got into my pyjamas and settled onto the sofa with Mum – BAM! The front door was busted wide open.

'What the *fuck*?' bellowed my mum, in her cockney accent. If it wasn't so tragic, I'd have been laughing. Kelly came belting into the room in floods of tears.

'Alex, *please*, please, it's not true!' she begged.

I couldn't square everything that had just happened

– Kelly's entrance, the domestic taking place in front of my mum, who technically was still pretending that Kelly was my 'friend'. It was all too much. When I'm angry, I find it difficult to talk – I have so much going on in my head, the words won't come out and I'm always terrified I'll end up like my dad, whose anger expressed itself in the most violent way possible. So instead, I go numb and lock down. I look like the coldest bitch on earth, but inwardly I'm just desperately trying to process everything.

Kelly was still repeating her appeal, alternating between denials and apologies.

At this point, I just wanted to move the situation away from my poor mum's house, so we grabbed Bailey, Kelly's dog, and headed back to hers.

In the end, we made up and just carried on. And guess what? We were happy, eventually buying our own house in December 2007. I'd found myself back in my laundry job at Arsenal trying to earn some extra money alongside playing in order to scrape together a deposit to buy the house with Kelly. I was always determined to split things 50/50 with her, even though she earned triple the money I did at that stage. Life was amazing. Kelly was settled; she'd bagged a job as Assistant Manager at the Arsenal Academy which gave her the routine she craved. Her addiction was still present but even looking back now, all I remember of this period was happiness and love. The only dark cloud was the difference I noticed between Kelly and me at work. As the star of English women's football, even in the latter stages of her career, Kel was treated as if she had this golden aura around her. She deserved it – but it meant that as her partner, sometimes I felt like people were using me to get to her talent. One member of staff at the Academy made my hackles rise in particular. This coach had a real way with words that I applaud to this day – she would feed my confidence, telling me I was going to be the best right back in the world. But I knew deep down that she was more interested in how Kelly might be of use to her future career plans and she wanted me onside because of that. It rubbed me up the wrong way and I kept her at arm's length, knowing she had other intentions.

Despite that, life continued, including training for the 2007 World Cup. It was England's first appearance for twelve years. Kelly and I both had an amazing tournament, even though the team made it no further than the quarter-finals (knocked out by America, a power-house team). Everyone finally got to see Kelly on a world stage as the superstar player she was, and I put myself on the map as a real asset in this exciting new-look England side – a right back who could defend and attack.

It was at this time the announcement was made about the new professional women's league in America. Kelly was in high demand. She was having none of it, however, thinking her time in America had been and gone. Emma Hayes – Arsenal's assistant coach – was announced as the Chicago Red Stars franchise manager. She spoke to me about how great it would be to play in America and go fully professional. It wasn't hard to see the positives – the first chance to go pro and get more than the few hundred a week I was on at Arsenal. My England contract was my main income at that point, as our salaries had been bumped up to £16,000, achieved after a long fight by Hope with the FA for investment. But Emma kept talking about drafting me and Kelly to Chicago. She knew Kelly would do anything for me, and that if I really wanted to play in America, Kelly would follow me. I felt like her real target was Kelly and I was being used as a pawn. It went against everything I'd strived for – I always want to attain things on my own merit.

That was when I got the call from Tony DiCicco. I was buzzing – even more so when Tony added that he was also planning to draft my teammate, Kelly Smith, to Boston but she'd told him her life was set in England. Because of the American rules, they'd have to draft her first round regardless, to stop other teams from doing so. All I heard was that Tony had no clue about my relationship with Kelly – he wanted me based solely on my talent. And in turn, I wanted to go. Kelly and I began talking seriously about moving to America. It would be different this time, I told her. I'd be with her. She was adamant she did not want to go to Chicago, but she really liked the thought of being in Boston, with me.

When the time for the draft announcements rolled around, we were away on England duty and had just finished dinner with the team. We were all eagerly following events via the web. I was so nervous; Boston had first pick and, like everyone expected, they selected Kelly. Great – now we were just waiting for me to be drafted to Boston in round three. Round three arrived, I saw my name, but . . . wait, what? Alex Scott drafted to . . . Chicago Red Stars?

I had told Emma I wasn't going to Chicago. I felt like it wasn't me she really wanted; she was just trying to get me there so that Kelly would follow. Why would Emma try and jeopardise my dream and my chance of playing in the WPS . . . ? It was a great big game that I was stuck in the middle of, and it was only later that I would find out the reason. Emma went on to tell Boston that Kelly and I were together, and she knew that Kelly would follow me to Boston, which meant they would have one of the best players in the world. But if they didn't take me, then they wouldn't have Kelly, so they would have to come up with a good package and deal to get me there. It wasn't messing with Kelly's dream, though – she was already a star player. Kel was moving there for me.

I'll spare you the months of wrangling it took to get me to Boston. After Emma finally accepted she would never be getting Kelly on the Red Stars, a deal was struck, and that was it – at the age of twenty-three, I was off to finally get paid just for playing football. My new salary of £45,000 was more money than I'd ever imagined earning in my life – and it was still less than the stars I was going to be surrounded by. But I didn't care; my foot was in the door and I was going to Boston with the love of my life. Could things get any better?

To this day, I say the three years Kelly and I spent in America were the happiest of our relationship. For the first time, we felt properly liberated, living in a beautiful apartment in a fun, diverse city. Our teammates were our friends – I'd never been part of a team which genuinely felt like a happy family, rather than a somewhat dysfunctional one. Our relationship flourished too. Which is why it might sound confusing when I tell you that Boston was where we had our third almost-break-up – and this one nearly stuck.

Every month, Kelly and I had to travel back to England – we had the 2009 Euros, followed by the 2011 World Cup qualifiers, so the matches were stacking up. On one particular visit, Tony had granted us permission to stay a little longer, so we could attend the end-of-season England awards. Kelly wasn't a fan of these events, but I'd persuaded her to come along as I really wanted to spend some time with my England teammates away from the pitch and have some fun. Heading to the after-party, I held my breath – in previous years, everyone had been off their faces. I wasn't drinking much, to support Kelly, and she seemed to be doing OK – she wasn't getting drunk, and every time I left her side to go off for a dance or a chat, she would whisper that she loved me. I felt on top of the world, and so lucky to have that kind of love.

But the evening turned sour. At some point, I excused

myself to go to the toilet. I remember walking into the cubicle and a teammate following me and asking me if Kel and I were all right, that she'd heard rumours and there was a lot of gossip about our relationship.

I felt like the air had been sucked out of the cubicle. I could hear my friend's voice, asking me what I was going to do. I had no idea what I was going to do. I had no idea there were any problems for me to deal with. I thought we were fine and had felt on cloud nine five minutes ago. And the idea that other people, that everyone knew about this before me – I was heartbroken.

There's a lot you have to stomach in relationships. I don't think love by its nature has to be painful but I definitely went about it the hard way. I didn't have a model of a healthy, happy relationship to follow. When things were good, they were wonderful. When they were bad, I wasn't sure what to do, or how to address either Kelly's or my own part in it. I didn't know how to open up. Both of us could be defensive as a protective measure. When you look back, with older, wiser, more forgiving eyes, you can see the cracks, but also the missed opportunities for understanding. I loved Kelly wholeheartedly and she felt the same about me, but at times we could both be so immature with our feelings or get caught up in the notions of what we thought was love that we could be so unkind to one another. I didn't always feel respected. I'm not sure what she would say about me. But this is my story, so all I can recount is that during our bad patches, I felt every bit the senior in the partnership, even though I was technically the junior in age, earnings and the respect I was afforded. That night of our blow-up, when my teammates told me the gossip about me and Kel, what had been going on behind my back, I experienced a mix of anger, shame and embarrassment. I wanted to hate her with a passion but I somehow couldn't. I wanted to vanish or for the ground to swallow me up. I didn't know how to deal with my world being turned upside down, and my feelings crescendoed into a horrible climax.

Afterwards, someone told Hope I was crying and she came to check on me while my teammates shared what had happened. 'I need to get out of here,' I thought – I hated the idea that people were talking about me. I won't recount the whole back-and-forth between Kelly and me, but it was endless shouting through tears and anger from us both. I felt what we had was broken forever. The tears wouldn't stop coming out; my heart felt broken.

I went where I've always gone when I'm in pain: Mum's. I got changed and immediately headed out on one of the longest walks I'd ever done with Ella, the little Boxer pup Kelly had bought me, to try and plan my next steps. I didn't want to be around Kelly. I couldn't think of her without having all these emotions come up that I didn't know how to deal with. The one thing I've always carried is my pride. She knew that. How could she do that to me when she knew how I felt about honesty, about the threat of abandonment? Some people might not have seen it as a big deal. Fair enough; I did. This was my first love and it was earth-shattering. The strength I thought I had now turned to insecurity and the trust was gone for the rest of our relationship.

Because, yes, we got back together. It took weeks. We both returned to Boston, and Kelly stayed with our team-mate, Heather Mitts, just upstairs from our flat. Training together was almost the easy part; from a young age I'd learned to switch off my emotions when it came to football. It had always been my space, free of everything going on outside, so I put on a brave face, not wanting the team to think we were disrupting them with personal issues. Kelly was a shell of herself, though. She had visibly lost weight, looked sad and had gone back to being the old Kelly: turn up to training, don't talk to anyone and go home. Heather told me she was drinking all the time and not eating.

'Alex, she's distraught,' she said.

I worried about her constantly, that it was my fault she was drinking again because I'd left her. The guilt I carried was immense. People around us were worried too. We had an important match coming up. Hope phoned me a few days before for a catch-up, and at the end of the call she casually dropped that she was coming over to watch the game too. That match was one of those situations where I wonder how I would have learned to handle life without the discipline football taught me. I had a fantastic game. The way I win is to keep thriving. I saw Hope in the bar after the match. She said that day, football came second. Yes, I'd had a good game, but she was there to support me as Alex Scott the person, not the footballer. I didn't know at the time how to articulate how much that meant to me; because of that I'm not sure I ever told Hope. So here it is: thank you, Hope.

I always thought that – having grown up with a father who disrespected my mother – I would stand firm once I'd made the decision that I couldn't fully trust someone to have my back. But guess what? Things are never that black and white. You can't predict how you're going to react to something until it actually happens to you. Every night, Kelly would knock on my apartment door and beg me to take her back. After a few weeks of this, I let her in. I won't detail what we discussed that night. It was enough that I forgave her. I couldn't forget about it – the incident remained a niggling voice in my head – but I chose to take her back. My love for Kelly was still there.

Just like that, we were a unit again – and we stayed like that for the next two years, until the WPS league underwent a massive restructure, with talk of it possibly folding. Boston Breakers was not going to be the same environment we'd loved so much, and with a home Olympics on the horizon, it seemed the right time to accept Vic Akers' offer to return to Arsenal and help the club in their next phase. So we did. Back to the home we'd built in those early happy days. But we were both struggling with our return to the UK, and to the tightly controlled footballing environment with much less pay.

The London 2012 Olympics should have been one of the highlights of my life. As a footballer, you don't often dream of playing in the Games, but 2012 was the first time Team GB would be competing. For it to be round the corner from where I'd grown up as a kid in Poplar was so unbelievably special. On the footballing side, I have amazing memories. We had massive crowds following us that tournament – it felt like the momentum from our run in the 2011 World Cup had gone to the next level. But when it came to my relationship, something had quietly changed. I was tired of feeling like I had to look after Kelly, especially when people would come to me during the Games and tell me to sort out her drinking. I can't speak for Kelly, but I think she was experiencing the same fatigue. I loved her so much, but that night at the awards had planted a seed of insecurity and nothing had quite been the same since. Every now and then I wanted to see her in the sort of pain I felt she had caused me. I would withdraw, transform into the Ice Queen, make her think that I was going to up and leave at a moment's notice. It was cruel. But I wanted her to feel the hurt and sadness that I did. I'd prided myself on not being a petty person. But I was also young and, at times, impulsive. Kelly, despite her age, often acted with immaturity too. Maybe it's the sheltered world of sports. We grow up in clubs from our childhood. I think, deep down, I knew there was a whole breadth of life experience I hadn't been able to tap into and learn from as an elite athlete. I yearned for it and Kel didn't so much.

Looking back, I can see I was broken, and that a relationship once filled with so much love had become tainted and sad. Hurt people hurt people. And that's what we did to each other. Along with that, she was tired of me constantly trying to stop her drinking and having a 'good time'. In interviews, she said her addiction was under control and maybe believed it herself. But it wasn't.

When the end came, I knew it was final, precisely because it was so anti-climactic. It was just an ordinary day in 2013. Kelly walked into the living room where I was chilling and said we needed to talk. I felt what was coming and had, in some strange way, been waiting for her to say the words. But I was still scared. She was eight years of my life, my first love.

'Alex, I think we need to split up,' she said.

I felt hot tears coming as I tried to choke out the words 'I think so too'. And just like that, eight years was over. What ended us wasn't my communication issues, or Kelly's drinking. We had both changed, and now we'd gone from growing together to stopping each other from being who we truly wanted to be. I had such a passion to explore, to step outside my comfort zone. Kelly was the opposite; she'd done that and needed routine and structure. I was chafing at the bit; she was fed up with feeling like she was holding me back.

Kelly moved out straight away. I had no idea how to process how I was feeling. For eight years I'd had this amazing comfort blanket and now I was alone. I didn't really know who I was either; I'd spent most of my twenties not living a life typical of mates my own age. Now it was just me and the dog, with a house I didn't know if I could afford to pay for. I lost a lot of weight without noticing, to the point where people were worriedly asking about it. Outwardly I didn't look stressed, but it was clear the circumstances were taking their toll. Yet typical Alex survival mode kicked in – I threw myself back into football and started planning for a future beyond it. I felt as though Kelly had, in a way, let me go, to explore a path outside of being pushed into a coaching role.

It's funny how life works. I don't live with regrets – there's truly nothing about this chapter with Kelly I would change. We helped each other grow as people and then, when the time was right, we set each other free. Kelly is now married with two children, and every time I see her, I love hearing about how happy she is and what's going on in her life. We're such different people now that it almost seems laughable that we'd have ever dated, or been so well-matched at the time. But we were.

If I'm honest, I have never trusted in a relationship since Kels. I've been scared of getting hurt again – and hurting someone in turn. It's only in the last few years, since starting therapy, that I've let myself slow down and process the pain. I'd tried to plaster over it by just throwing myself into the next project, the next challenge. But I hadn't healed, and all my subsequent relationships suffered. Not everyone subscribes to this, but for me, the saying that you can't give love if you don't love yourself rings extremely true.

When I've done interviews or been on dates over the past few years, people have often asked, 'Why are you single?' If it was a date, I'd tell them the truth: I didn't know. But now I understand that I needed time and space to break the patterns of my past. This has taken a different kind of strength, and so much of it.

For the first time since Kelly, I can feel myself ready to love again, with all the deep connection and vulnerability of that relationship, but without repeating some of the cycles that I'd unwittingly participated in first time round. I've grown and matured. I'm open to receiving love. I have been closed off for a very long time now. But after coming out of my last relationship, I knew I had to work on myself to get to the point where I could give someone else all of me, and be there in the way they deserve. And here I am.

8

Strength Is . . .
Listening To Your Gut

When I give talks, I often speak about comfort zones. I'm someone who's always been scared of staying there. It's a space of complacency, of cruising rather than pushing forward. It comes from an early fear of losing my place in a team and what that could lead to. In my head, there was always the thought that I needed to be better than I was yesterday so I wouldn't be replaced.

This might not be the healthiest motivation in the world but it's worked. I get told I'm 'grounded' quite a lot, and this mentality is where that comes from – I know that whatever is going on in my life, it could all end tomorrow if I'm not doing what's necessary. I've always loved the quote 'Hard work beats talent when talent doesn't work hard'; it speaks to me because I've never considered myself the *best* when it comes to talent alone. But whatever I turn my hand to, people around me know I will give everything I have to offer. And when I no longer feel like I am prepared to do that, well . . . then I know it's time for a change.

In 2012, thoughts about life after football started to

A rare family photo of the four of us.

Ronnie and me getting into the
festive spirit.

Dad, Ronnie and me –
Daddy's little girl.

Mum, Ronnie and me showing off the football trophies he had just collected.

Young Arsenal youth team days, in our Centre of Excellence training kit.

My best friend Regan and me on holiday in the Dominican Republic. She's braided her hair to try to be like me.

England Youth
U16s camp.

Working in the
Arsenal laundry when
one day my favourite
Ian Wright popped in
to say hello. I was
sixteen or seventeen
years old.

On tour with the
Arsenal Ladies in
Oklahoma.

2007: holding onto that Champions League trophy after we had just won.

Kelly and me, in Boston, 2010.

My favourite moment with Arsenal: winning the FA Cup Final at Wembley in 2016.

Team GB at the London Olympics, when we had just beaten Brazil at Wembley.

Retirement from the England team and being honoured at the next game. Mum and Skye were with me as I took it all in.

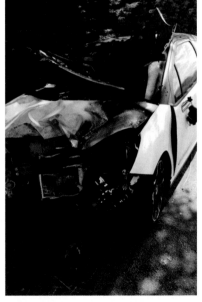

That car crash in 2014. The ambulance drivers had no idea how I'd survived with nothing more than a scratch.

Nan, Mum and Skye at the Palace with me as I collected my MBE.

I used to sit for hours with my nan in this very room and talk about anything and everything, or sometimes just sit together in silence.

A happy moment, when I finally got to take Mum to Wimbledon for a day out.

My baby Ella, the most precious gift I could have ever asked for.

Louise Sutton, my friend, my mentor, and someone who has been there from the very start of my broadcasting career.

A rare birthday celebration with some of my closest friends.

A history-making moment as I became the first female pundit for the BBC at a Men's World Cup.

Sam Barks, Jason Gardiner and me, celebrating the last day of filming after a long, gruelling two weeks.

Working alongside two presenters I have admired for years is 'pinch me' kind of stuff.

Me in my new career and loving what I do.

creep into my mind. I'd been in America for the past three years and my perspective on life was irreversibly changed. My eyes had been opened to the world – and new pursuits. While playing for the Boston Breakers, I would write weekly blogs, updating fans on funny stories and insights into life as a professional footballer. These were hugely popular – I began to receive more and more messages on social media from people telling me they loved these posts. This feedback sparked something inside of me and I took it one step further, beginning to film team challenges on my GoPro at the end of practice sessions. I loved being able to share the real, lively personalities of my teammates with fans; it always confused me how, in post-match interviews, I would see the funny and carefree people I knew suddenly freeze and become wooden as soon as they were put in front of a camera.

The response I got to these videos was great – they clearly helped build a more personal connection between players and fans. So I started doing the same while on England duty. Instead of sitting in my room watching a box set, I would hang around the FATV (Football Association TV) guys Damian Cullen and Joe Bennett, learning the basics of how equipment and editing processes worked. Eventually I asked them if I could film on the GoPro – this became #SCOTTIECAMS, which are still up on YouTube today. I knew the fans had an appetite for more than basic interviews after games. Instead we could give them insights into training, behind-the-scenes footage of things like our camp diet, and so on. It seemed so simple to me, but it wasn't being done back then. I even started filming when I was away from camp so people could continue the journey with me and see a glimpse of my life and personality outside of football. These clips were different to anything being done in my part of the sporting world at the time and I was loving the chance to be creative. It's funny that this sort of insider access is the norm now; teams post everything from behind-the-scenes clips to memes on their social media accounts to allow fans extra insight into players' lives. Fans can connect to players more than ever, and in turn this gives players the freedom to be more human. To see players like Danny Rose, in Gareth Southgate's 2018 Men's World Cup squad, speak so openly about his struggles with mental health was very powerful.

All this camerawork had me thinking. Post-America, Hope Powell wanted me to get my coaching badges, a standard path for elite footballers to follow at the tail end of their playing career, especially as Hope was such an advocate for trying to push for more female coaches coming through. She didn't want all that knowledge to be wasted. When Hope was playing, former pros had to retrain in a completely different field once their playing days were over. Karen Walker, who once held the record as England's top women's goal scorer, went to work as a postie when she was done. Now don't get me wrong, I also did postie shifts, working nights at the Watford Post Office during the Christmas and New Year period when saving for the deposit for our house. It was tough work, especially as I would get home at 9am, grab a couple of hours' sleep, then head off to the Arsenal laundry. There were occasions when I wanted to fall over, I was that tired, but I never let anyone see just how fatigued I was, except Kelly. Now Hope was adamant that players could, and would, have roles within football if they got the qualifications needed.

I started on my badges but knew that coaching wasn't my passion. I couldn't see myself doing it as a full-time job – it just wouldn't make me happy. I was doing it for the sake of it, which is a trap I never wanted to fall into. I was looking around for another option at the same time as the Professional Football Association (PFA) had taken the first step to include the FA Women's Super League (WSL). If female players signed up to be PFA members they would be granted the same benefits that the men had. To be honest, most of the players didn't have a clue what they were signing up for. The PFA would tour clubs, giving an hour-long whirlwind of a presentation, encouraging people to pay the £100 member's fee, using the example of how PFA insurance would cover you if you suffered a career-ending injury. The part that stood out for me was the PFA's offer to fund university courses. This part was always skimmed over; no examples were on offer of exactly what courses were eligible for PFA funding, or which former players had benefited from the grant. You were just waved away to 'find all the information on the website'. Most people didn't bother doing this. But I was at my wits' end, really worrying about what my life after football would look like, even though I was in the prime of my career and had potentially seven years of playing left. I knew I had to start putting the wheels in motion. Who would want to employ a female footballer without any real qualifications behind her? My survival mode was strong.

I sat scrolling on the PFA's website, looking at the courses they offered. Then I found it, in small, hard-to-read text: 'Sign up to the Professional Sports Writing and Broadcast Media degree at Staffordshire University and the PFA can help with your funding and manage it alongside your professional playing career.' My eyes lit up. This was it, the course I was meant to do. If I wanted to try and get into this field, I needed to do it the right way, through studying and learning all the skills necessary. Arsenal couldn't really say no, to be honest – they'd been banging on for years about how important it was for players to get an education alongside their footballing career. And here I was, asking for nothing from them, no financial support, no time off training, just permission to do it. I'd done all the research so I could present the idea to Arsenal and show them my studies wouldn't interfere with playing; I'd only have to miss one session a month to attend classes and could do a double day to make up for it, so no one could complain I was getting special treatment. The PFA had agreed that upon completion of the course, they would fund half of its cost.

The course started in September 2013. I was twenty-eight

years old, and so excited that I started telling other players about my plans. A few days after I had told some of the team, Emma Byrne said, 'Reens, I've signed up for that course you're doing, so we can do it together.' I looked at her, surprised, but replied, 'Oh great.' I was trying to work out why she would want to do it. She was already working as a goalkeeping coach at the Arsenal Academy, which she had done for a year, and had never expressed any interest in this other field. But I figured it was like when people join a gym and feel more confident when they have a mate go to a class with them. I wasn't there just to get a qualification though. I knew from the moment I signed up that this was going to be my next career. I was determined to make it happen. I didn't even know where Staffordshire University was, but no matter what, I would get there once a month.

I started putting extra money aside so I always had enough petrol to get me there and back, and calculated how Emma and I could go halves and take it in turns to drive. In the event, it actually worked out better to get the train, but I was *committed* to making this happen. The week before the course started, I went to WH Smith and stocked up on pens, pads and highlighters, trying to think what stuff university kids needed to buy. I had been out of the school system for so long, I didn't know how it all worked. I had no idea what an NUS card was, and how you could use it to get discounts. I found this out way too late and, besides, was always in the mindset of 'I'm surviving, I'm not in debt, so I don't need to ask for discounts'. Duh – of course you should take advantage of discounts if they're there! If the opportunity to save money presents itself, take it!

The first day of the course arrived and I was full of nerves. Emma and I immediately got lost on campus and had to ask for directions to our classroom. We'd received quite a few emails in the run up to the course beginning, detailing log-ins and online materials, but it was a lot of information all at once and I knew I just needed to speak to someone in person to understand everything. Old fears were rearing their heads too: what if I had to read out loud? Or write things on the board that I wouldn't be able to spell? What if I looked stupid in front of my new classmates? These thoughts played on loop in my mind as Emma and I walked around campus. The buildings reminded me of school; they were old and dated compared to vibrant London. I felt like I had stepped back in time. Five minutes late, we eventually made it through the campus maze and stepped into class. Immediately I clocked our classmates were all men and remembered – of course, we were doing this through the PFA, which has historically been men only. Emma and I were the first women to sign up for a course, apparently. We hurried in and found a seat, then I took in the people around me and spotted a familiar face.

A couple of months prior, I'd been at a footballing function and was introduced to Fabrice Muamba, the former Bolton Wanderers midfielder. He had the biggest smile I'd ever seen and seemed so happy the whole time.

He'd retired the year before, after suffering a heart attack on the field. I remember watching on TV as it happened – one of the most harrowing things I'd ever seen. It changed football; the game was not prepared or equipped to deal with anything like Fabrice's collapse. It took a Tottenham Hotspur fan in the crowd, cardiologist Dr Andrew Deaner, to run on to the pitch and save Fabrice's life. Incredibly, Fabrice survived – but he could no longer play football. Instead, he was on this media course with me, trying to find a life after his sporting career.

When I sat down, Fabrice smiled and said, 'Alex, it's good to see you.'

'You too, Fab,' I replied. It felt comforting to already know someone on the course. There were only about eight of us in total, and every month that dwindled further to a few regular faces who showed up consistently. From the start, I was fully aware I had to prove to people around me how dedicated I was to my degree if I wanted them to recognise I was serious about a potential career in media. So that's what I did. Training at Arsenal was now up to three times a week – even though the women's game was still not fully professional – but on my days off, I would complete the hours of work placements that were required for my course. I contacted Sky Sports, who agreed I could spend two weeks at their headquarters in west London. I was so keen to take everything in and learn as much as I could, so I could tell which parts I really loved and where my skill set would be best suited. My first week was spent writing various sports articles for the website and learning how producers directed shows from the galleries (the production control room). That was my first real understanding of the monster machine that goes into making a show, especially a live one.

After learning what went on in the gallery, I spent a few days sitting alongside Natalie Sawyer, studying her presenting techniques, how she read the autocue. Timing is a major issue; as much as you might want to stay talking about one subject, it doesn't work like that. You usually have to hit a number of different features or news bulletins within a set period of time. There's also advertising breaks. On top of that, the presenter has to let their guest say their piece, listen to what they're saying *and* register the instructions being passed to them by up to three different voices in their ear. Sky gave me an earpiece like Natalie's, so I could hear all the different directions she was getting, while simultaneously having to deliver the show. All this was fascinating to me.

These placements could often be an eye-opener in different ways. One time I was working at the FA, sitting in on press conferences for team announcements. I remember being there for Roy Hodgson announcing the 2013 England squad at Wembley. I had played at Wembley in the 2012 Olympics; it was a stadium I'd dreamed about when running around the football cage as a kid. And here I was, at Wembley on my work placement in a brand-new context. At first, walking into the press conference room, I felt so lucky. I was used to watching squad announcements on Sky Sports News while at home, and now I was in the very space where they happened. The room itself isn't exactly grand and historic. It's filled with red chairs, and at the front there's a table in front of sheeting, filled with the logos of brands sponsoring the team. Roy sat behind the table, with mics and cameras set up ready for recording. I was just there to observe and take notes on what sort of questions were being asked and how Roy was responding. All the waiting journalists knew me as Alex Scott the footballer, so they didn't seem to think it strange I was there. But I was Alex Scott the intern, and it opened my eyes. I was the only woman in the room full stop, let alone the only Black woman, surrounded by a group of white men over forty. If I'm honest, I hadn't really thought about this before – I existed in the world of women's football, and while I was very aware of the inequalities that permeated the game and the media circus around it, I hadn't seen the stark evidence in front of me of how deep that went. At the end of the press conference, I heard a voice call my name.

'Alex, hello! I'm Glenn Moore from the *Independent*. I've been across your career for a number of years now, it's good to see you here. What are you up to, if you don't mind me asking?'

I explained to Glenn about my degree.

'—so I'm trying to learn everything I can,' I finished.

Glenn always had this warm, soft smile on his face. You can tell straight away that he's a friendly guy.

'That's really great to hear,' he said. 'Look, here's my business card. If you want any work experience in this side of things, drop me a message.'

'Thanks, Glenn, I really appreciate it,' I said. 'I'll be in touch.'

Was Glenn ahead of the game that day? Did he see what I saw in that room: the complete absence of women? Was he thinking he could be part of changing that? Or was he just responding to a player he knew and offering a helping hand?

Elsewhere, I'd also begun to think it was strange that I was heading off to placements at sports broadcasting organisations when I could be learning from the place I called home: Arsenal. The women's department obviously knew I was doing this degree, but no one had reached out to me about it, so I took matters into my own hands. Through some digging, I tracked down the guys who worked at Arsenal TV and asked if I could come along on days off to learn from them. They were buzzing as they'd never had a player take an interest in that side of things before. Personally, I think there would have been a lot of players keen to get involved but it just wasn't what was done back then. We existed in a rigidly controlled environment and never dreamed we'd be allowed to do stuff like that – or that we could use the spare time we did have to get more involved with this side of the club. On the women's team, the old saying 'you should be seen and not heard' hung over us like a spectre. There was a fear that we shouldn't be seen to ask for too much, that we were lucky to have as much as we already did. But as time went on and I matured as an individual, I understood this didn't need to be the case. Our club ethos was for Arsenal to lead the way in women's football, to always try to be the example rather than a follower. Arsenal taught me that – so why would it not apply in this case?

In 2014, the toll of such a physical career was also pushing me further to consider a future beyond it. During one Arsenal game that year, I received a serious kick to the head. The medics bandaged me up and I ran back on to the pitch. I had a splitting headache but tried to push past the pain, managing to finish out the game. That evening, a few of the girls and I went for dinner and a few glasses of wine. As designated driver, I said I could drop three of the others home. My head was pounding but it was nothing a good night's sleep wouldn't cure, I thought. One by one, I dropped all my passengers off and began the last leg of my drive.

Next thing I knew, I was being brought round in an ambulance. I had blacked out; that headache had actually been a delayed-onset concussion. My little car had travelled over two roundabouts and smashed up against a lamppost, with – apparently – a huge bang. Luck was on my side, though. I had crashed right next to a Travellers' site in Hertfordshire. Two of them had heard the impact of my car colliding with the lamppost and came to my rescue, hauling me out of the wreckage before the car went up in flames and ringing emergency services – police, fire brigade and paramedics – from my phone. When I woke up, they'd gone – two angels who had been sent in that moment to save me. The ambulance men were in shock; they had no idea how I'd survived with nothing more than a scratch from my seat belt. I was in a daze; all I wanted was to go to bed.

'Please, I just want to go home,' I told a policeman as we waited for my breathalyser results.

When they came up negative, I finally got my wish, with a police car as my taxi. I went to sleep like nothing had happened. The next day, I was off to an England camp. I pointed out the site of my crash to my driver, who was a regular. He must have told one of the England bosses because I got a call from our team doctor, asking if I'd been in a car crash.

'Don't worry, doc, I'm totally fine,' I said, laughing it off. All I was thinking was, 'I have to go and play for England. I can't let them down.' That's what I did. We played against Sweden two days later and I had a great game, bombing up and down the wing. But the emotional side is all a bit of a blur. I didn't let myself really feel the trauma of the incident. And it prompted another shock; Mum was in bits about the thought of losing me. For the first time in years, she got on the phone to my dad in a state of anger to tell him he'd nearly lost me to a car crash and he'd been granted a second chance by the heavens to be a presence in my life. He showed up with his then girlfriend to watch my England game and I went to meet him in the players' bar after the Sweden game. I was still numb from the crash and found myself coming straight off the pitch, to twist on an uncomfortable bar stool and make small talk with a man who hadn't been around for years. It was too much to even try to comprehend. But on some level my mind was clearly registering the impact.

We had another England game scheduled in a few days, in the south of the country, which required heading down on the team bus. I always sat in the same seat during these journeys, with Fara Williams in front of me. Getting on the coach that day, my chest felt tight. As the bus set off, I felt my throat begin to close up and my chest tightened. Suddenly, I was sobbing and trying desperately to gulp in air, while also hiding my face so no one else would notice what was happening – I was having a panic attack. Fara clearly heard me; she peered through the seat and a moment later, I heard her voice calling the doctor to come down the aisle. He sat down beside me and slowly ran me through some breathing exercises to calm me down. As soon as I could catch my breath again, I pleaded with him to just leave me alone.

'I'm fine,' I said, tears still tracking down my face. 'I will chill when we get to the hotel.'

There wasn't much he could do in the face of this and left me be. I really did believe that was all there was to the episode. It was just a wobble. I had to be fit to show up for the game. I couldn't let myself think about it.

Doing things off the pitch allowed me to escape those negative thoughts – and explore a whole new side of myself. Working with Arsenal TV was where I got my first practical experience of live broadcasting, with me in the hot seat. On match days I began to take on pundit duties, which quickly led to me being asked if I wanted to host the match games for Arsenal TV. Not only was I having a blast, it gave me all the work experience needed to complete my degree. I went above and beyond, not because I had to, but because I was loving everything I was doing. Not wanting to neglect any area of my new field, I also reached out to Glenn Moore at the *Independent*, who was all too happy to hear from me.

'Alex, I want you to do a column for the men's Euros, are you up for that?' he asked.

'Really?' I said. 'Like, my actual column will be in the paper?'

'Yes, if it's good enough,' he told me.

'Wow. Thank you, Glenn!'

He set out what he wanted from me. Every couple of days, I would write down my thoughts and analysis of the games played and send it to him via email. He would edit it, going through the spelling and grammar, re-arranging certain parts, then send it back to me. Writing these articles was so challenging, not because I didn't know what to write – that was the easy part, I could have done that super fast – but because I didn't want Glenn to think I was stupid, or to let on about being dyslexic. I would spend hours and hours trying to edit and spell check it before I even sent it. The day my first piece came out, I rang Mum.

'Mum, it's in the paper today!' I said, all excited. She rushed to the shop to grab a copy, ringing me back to let me know that there was even a little photo of me alongside my words. I was so grateful to Glenn for this opportunity (apparently the first time a female footballer in the UK had done a column covering a men's tournament). After the Euros finished, Glenn was very kind with his feedback. He also told me that in all his years as a newspaper journalist, I was only the second footballing figure to write their own words, the other being Rafa Benitez. Everyone else usually used a ghostwriter; all they needed to do was jump on the phone for ten minutes and answer a couple of questions. I smiled, feeling like the hard work and hours I was putting in would pay off.

The degree even helped with the footballing side of things – it gave me a focus outside of the game, which actually made me enjoy training more. I had really struggled to adjust to life back in England, going from being a 'professional' in America, with a caring team bond that I had yet to experience elsewhere, to a league that wasn't professional and wasn't properly compensated. Because of this, players in England had a different mentality. The motivation to push beyond a ceiling was not there. As I've recounted previously, in America team support meant pulling other players up with you, as Kristine Lilly had told me, and Heather Mitts had shown me with the extra drills she would run me through. But when I took this attitude back to Arsenal, it didn't go down as well – one player cried after training after I kept telling her that she was taking too many touches and should work on passing the ball quicker. Through tears, she told me she thought I didn't like her. It was the opposite, I said – if I didn't care, I wouldn't be investing time in telling her what she needed to hear to make the England team. But that wasn't the culture in England; I found I had to alter my approach to meet what the team needed, even if it was individually frustrating. So thankfully, my degree gave me somewhere to channel my restless energy.

People soon began to notice what I was doing with #SCOTTIECAMS. One day I got an email from a producer telling me he was working on a new show to sit alongside one of Sky's flagship programmes, *Soccer AM*. He thought I could be perfect for what they had in mind and asked if I could come in for a chat.

Well, this sounded amazing. I'd grown up glued to *Soccer AM* at weekends, and being asked into the Sky Sports studio where I had already completed a work placement was exciting, whatever happened. Once there I met Shane O'Brien, who explained that Sky were investing in more productions for digital platforms – the one I was testing for was for a YouTube show called *Soccer AM II* that would go out online via all Sky channels.

'Right,' he said. 'Let's take you into the studio and do a screen test.'

'Shit,' I thought, 'what's a screen test?' There was a brief moment of panic as I hadn't prepared, but I thought the best thing I could do was just be myself. So that's what I did. Alan Smith ('Smithy') was in the studio that day as he was lined up as co-presenter for whoever got the gig. We hit it off straight away and Shane loved it. After my screen test, he took me to another room and asked if I could play the role of dummy interviewee for a runner who had worked at Sky for years and was auditioning for the Monday night show. After the interview I told Shane that I thought the woman had been fantastic and that I'd really enjoyed the chat. He smiled, and Laura Woods went on to debut as a brand-new presenter on Sky Sports' Monday night YouTube show. Since then, Laura's been named Best Sports Presenter by the British Sports Journalism Awards two years in a row; and my career hasn't gone too badly either, with an RTS and a Guild award to my name!

From my work on that *Soccer AM 11* episode I think I earned about a couple of hundred pounds and was treated to a cheeky Nando's on the way home. I had an agent of sorts, named Matthew Buck, who worked at the PFA at the time. I'd looked to sign with him when I came back from America; I say 'looked' because Matt was very honest and told me straight up that I wasn't earning enough money to warrant him taking a cut. Instead he became an advisor to me; I had him look over my football contracts and act as a go-between for me and Arsenal as I knew I was being too soft. One

Monday night, as I was washing up at home, Matt called me.

'ITV have been in touch, chasing me about you,' he said. 'They want you to go in and film a pilot for some TV show. I don't think it's going to be anything much so I told them "no".'

'Hang on,' I replied. 'When is it?'

It transpired the pilot was being filmed next week, on my day off.

'I'm just going to go along and see what it's like,' I decided. 'What harm can it do?'

Matt laughed and said he'd inform ITV.

The following week I rocked up on my own to the ITV studios, with no information about what this was or who was involved. Well, when I opened the door and strolled in, I've never felt so shy (and actually a little embarrassed) – in front of me were Holly Willoughby, Frank Lampard, Bradley Walsh and Jimmy Bullard, all with entourages buzzing around them. And there was me, on my tod, thinking I must have walked into the wrong room. I hadn't; it turned out that ITV were hoping to launch this new game show. All I needed to do, a producer told me, was have fun. Which I did – Bradley Walsh was my team captain and he has the gift of making everyone feel special. After filming finished there were drinks downstairs; I went for one but felt so awkward being solo, while everyone else seemed to have friends and agents with them, that I quickly said my goodbyes and left.

Later that week I got a call from Jim Erwood, Jimmy Bullard's agent. He told me the pilot we'd filmed had got the green light and was going to be aired as the full-blown first episode of new series *Play to the Whistle*. Furthermore, Jim personally said ITV were buzzing with how I had come across, and he'd also been impressed by my performance and wanted to sign me as a client so he could help me with the TV side of things. 'Help with the TV side of things' was exactly what I needed, so we came to a mutual agreement to work together.

Everyone within football circles could see and hear about what I was doing, which made me particularly conscious of the need to never let my media work interfere with training. If I had the slightest off-day it could be used as fuel against me, to prove I lacked focus. I also saw my media work as aiding the promotion of women's football – every show I appeared on, I was billed as 'Alex Scott, Arsenal and England Women's football player'. I wasn't just representing myself, I was shining a light on our sport at a time when the women's side wasn't getting the most coverage. Once more, football was opening doors for me, just like a gut feeling had told me it would the moment I signed to Arsenal. Maybe this is the moment to say, I've always been a spiritual person. I'm not wedded to a single religion – even though I was raised a Christian and have a cross tattoo on my hand to remind me of being in touch with my spiritual side. It's not a Christian tattoo though; rather it represents being open to the universe, to the signs it sends, to the idea that there is something bigger than us humans present. And most of all it's being open to listening to that gut feeling and voice within, especially at times when I've wondered if the path I was on was the right one. But when I've put the trust in my gut and taken those leaps of faith, it has always worked out in the end. I don't have easy answers on how you can judge whether the voice within is speaking to you out of bravery or fear. There is no one-size-fits-all solution. But if that voice inside is piping up and you can find the courage to say yes to something, even if it might not work out exactly as planned – do it.

In 2015, I was off to a good start with my media work. I had *Soccer AM 11*, was hosting Arsenal TV match day shows and had started guesting on the *Women's Football Show* alongside Jacqui Oatley and Tina Daheley. I was even presenting a Thursday night show on London Live. Jim Erwood was beavering away in the background, trying to bring something my way. I had a goal: to be a presenter in the mould of Holly Willoughby, Clare Balding or Gabby Logan. You could see just how brilliant they were at their job, consistently top tier. I realised that while I might be a footballer now, when I looked to my future, that's where I wanted to be: as a footballer the goal was to be the best right back in the world, and in TV I was telling myself I wanted to do everything I could to be among the best. 'Top tier' is always the goal. People will have a preference for who they like the 'best', depending on personality or the shows they watch, but you need someone who can consistently deliver: that's being top tier. Once I had a conversation with my England teammate Leah Williamson, the night before she was due to play a World Cup qualifier. She said she didn't think she'd had a good performance in her last game because she hadn't 'done much'. I told her at international level, the key was to always play at a good level; that her game had been good because if there was a scale ranking performance from 0–10, she'd have been an eight. You need players in a team that you know, no matter what, will deliver you an eight or above when they're on the pitch. It's no good if one game you're a nine out of ten and the next you're a four. For me, being top tier, whether in football or TV, means always giving a performance at level eight and above.

Jim had fixed up meetings for me with two upcoming reality shows that were being cast. The first one was a bust; I knew within minutes of meeting the tall, blonde, larger-than-life casting agent who greeted us that I wasn't right for the programme, which I discovered was Channel 4's *The Jump*. Even though I was slightly relieved – the show involved risky skiing, which most elite athletes are contractually banned from doing as it can potentially result in career-ending injuries – I also felt crappy. What if I just wasn't the right sort of personality for this work? But there was no time to wallow – immediately it was on to the next meeting. Jim had told me very little about this one, only that it was a programme where I would be 'pushed hard'. Which would be easy, he said, as 'you're used to being pushed hard'. Little did we know! But within five minutes of sitting down I was praying the team would pick me – the show sounded like the most incredible adventure I would go on, in a part of the world I never could have imagined I'd get to visit: South Africa. Several calls (and one rejection from *The Jump*) later and it was official: I'd been picked as part of the cast for the adventure show *Bear Grylls: Mission Survive*, which would be broadcast to a prime-time audience on ITV.

I was buzzing with excitement, but the biggest hurdle lay ahead of me: how would I even ask Arsenal if I could go? Filming was scheduled for late October and I'd be gone for two weeks, totally off grid. No phone, nothing. I hoped management would see it my way; all I'd need was permission to miss training, and it would be the first time women's football was represented in the mainstream media outside of tournament season. Surely they had to see the benefits? Plus, the pay from the show would give me more leeway to play football. I'd get paid triple the amount for two weeks on *Bear Grylls* that I did all year playing for Arsenal. Still, the conversation with Clare Wheatley was one of the hardest I've ever had. Who likes feeling as if they're letting someone down? Not me. But that's how it felt, sitting in Clare's office, asking for permission. We chatted it through, however, and she took it to Pedro Martínez Losa, the new Arsenal Ladies manager, to clear it with the rest of Arsenal management. Thankfully, Pedro said yes and was genuinely excited for me. I was just allowing myself to believe that this really would happen when our football schedule changed – the FA Women's League Cup Final was suddenly rescheduled for mid-week, right when I was supposed to be in South Africa. Shit. Pedro and Clare told me I couldn't do the show, and I accepted it at first, even though my voice within was screaming at me that everything about this show was calling my name. But Jim was having none of me backing out.

'Alex, this is bigger than one final,' he told me. 'You could help put women's football on the map on a different level! You could drive change.' He was trying everything to persuade me, and even though I knew he was trying to butter me up a bit, he did have a point. ITV prime time was a totally different – and mainstream – audience. The FA Women's League Cup Final wasn't even going to be televised; it was taking place in a venue that meant most fans couldn't even make it, and it had been rescheduled without a second thought. I was becoming increasingly frustrated at things like this happening in women's football, and here I was being presented with an opportunity not only for myself but for women's football. Getting more eyes and attention on the game was everything we needed. I knew in my heart the decision I was going to make but had no clue how I was going to make it happen. I know it sounds cheesy but I really did think it was bigger than me. I kept picturing those little Alexes, the young girls playing football, who might see me on the TV and know they could follow their dreams. I had to make this happen.

I pleaded with Clare and Pedro (it also wasn't as easy to get out of the ITV contract as I'd expected, so that was another spanner in the dropping-out works). As captain, I knew I would be letting the team down in one way, but in another I'd be representing Arsenal Women on a massive platform. The team knew me, they knew what I was about. And when it came down to it, 98 per cent of the team supported me in doing the show (the other 2 per cent, well . . . I won't name names but they tried to have the captain's armband stripped from me. Sadly for them, democracy won).

To cut a long story – and lots of begging – short, management relented, and I found myself being snuck through a secret back entrance into Heathrow Airport so no one would clock on. Walking through the door, I got the same rush of nerves as I had doing the *Play to the Whistle* pilot. I was greeted by the eight other celebrities signed up. Stuart Pearce spotted me and immediately picked up on my fear. 'Don't worry, kid!' he told me kindly, 'I'll look after you!' A coach to the core. I also quickly hit it off with a girl named Samantha Barks, who was so normal and down to earth – I had no idea she was a big theatre star. We're still really good mates to this day. And then I was on the plane and, without knowing it, on to the next chapter of my life.

Doing *Bear Grylls* was a turning point. I went in as Alex Scott the footballer and came out as Alex Scott, full stop. I realised I needed to stop viewing myself as this one thing. Society encourages us to place ourselves, and others, in neat little boxes. You're expected to remain there and it takes real courage to break out and do something else. Even now, people tell me I do *so* much, in slightly disapproving tones. I'm interested in lots of different things; I'm never going to box myself in. That's something to take forward – if you have the space, explore all sides of yourself. 'Success is not final. Failure is not fatal. It's the courage to continue that counts.' Bear Grylls recited that Winston Churchill quote while on the show.

Even with all the time spent thinking about it, I was not quite prepared for what I was about to put my mind and body through. And even if I had known, I'm not sure there is any kind of training you can do that prepares you to face your fears. I've never been a strong swimmer and I'm scared of heights. Imagine combining both those fears into one terrifying task. Not a day went by when I wouldn't tell myself, 'I don't think I can do this. I'm going to be sent home today. I'm going to have to say no.' The first challenge we were set was the easiest for me: hiking with a massive backpack, filled with all our clothes, equipment and food for the show. Poor Chelsee Healey, bless her – the bag was bigger than she was. As we started hiking she kept falling over. Chelsee had been called off standby (someone who fills in if one of the original cast drops out) and had gone from being in her bikini in a nice little South African hotel, to full-on hiking gear and muddy boots. After falling a couple of times, Chelsee turned to me and said, 'Al, this ain't for me, y'know. I'm not going to be able to do this, watch, I'll be the first booted off, I can't even carry my backpack.' At first we laughed, but after two hours hiking in the blistering heat, among the mountains of South Africa, with no clue how long we were doing this for, Chelsee's laughter turned to tears. Stumbling along, she said, 'I just can't . . . I'm not going to be able to do it.'

'Chels,' I replied, 'just make it to base camp and we'll see what happens.'

An hour more and we ground to a halt. Before leaving, Bear had told us a story about his adventures and being lost in baking hot conditions. He'd said sometimes the only way to survive if you had no water was to drink your own pee (something Bear is famous for). We all looked at each other. Now it made sense why, on the first day of our arrival at our first little base camp, we'd been told to provide a urine sample. A big sample at that. Here we were, four hours into this trek, being handed back the bottles with our own wee in, being made to drink it as the first task. I looked around; some of the guys' samples were rank. Yuk. Being in athlete mode, I was used to drinking loads, so at the time of the sample I was very hydrated, and mine was not far off the transparency of water, which made this task the easiest for me. I opened the flask and downed my own wee, as you do. I honestly don't know how some of the others did though, because theirs stank.

Things got harder from there. Every morning we would wake up, with no clue about what lay ahead. In the second episode, I had to pull myself between two cliffs via a single rope, with my huge backpack on. Knowing my fear of heights, Bear made me go first. Before I even touched the rope, I was shaking with nerves. Bear was shouting at me from the opposite cliff. 'Come on, Alex! You're used to leading! Lead by example!' All I could manage to yell back was: 'OK, Bear!' I didn't care at all what he was saying. I was that terrified, I could only really hear myself. 'Come on, Alex,' I told myself. 'You can do this.' I kept thinking that I couldn't give up because then I would embarrass myself, and the whole reason for me pushing to be on this show was bigger than me – it was to give women's football a platform. I *had* to do this. Slowly, painfully, I started pulling myself across the rope, trying desperately not to flick my eyes downward and clock how high I was. To paint a picture of just how high up we actually were, it was above the clouds. Suddenly I felt myself shaking through nerves. I couldn't stop the rope quivering and – BAM! Just like that I went from crawling along the top of the rope to hanging on for dear life underneath. I was stuck.

'What do I do now?' I muttered.

I heard Bear's voice. 'You're going to have to do it the hard way, Alex,' he shouted. 'You'll need to use every bit of strength to pull yourself across.'

Already dripping in the South African heat and feeling exhausted, I took a deep breath and started trying to pull myself across. My arm muscles were beginning to cramp and, to make matters worse, the GoPro camera on my chest had caught on the rope. It was blocking the way for me to continue. I wanted to cry.

'You can do it, Alex,' instructed Bear. 'Let go of the rope with one of your hands and move it.'

'Absolutely not,' I thought. 'If I let go with one of my hands, I'll fall. My arms are already too weak from having to hold on for dear life and haul myself along.'

Then I remembered an incident the day before. It had been one of our first big challenges and I'd got myself into a bit of bother. We'd been paired up and made to abseil down a long rope. Halfway down, we'd had to unclip our backpacks and reattach them to a different part of the rope, which required working with your partner. My partner and I had successfully attached the first bag but as we dangled in mid-air and passed the second over, it started to slip out of my partner's hand. Somehow, I managed to scoop the 30kg backpack on to my foot. It hung on the edge of my ankle and I had no way of getting it back into my partner's hand. We completed the rest of the challenge with this bag in the most dramatic of positions, knowing at any moment it might drop into oblivion. Looking back, it made for great TV, but when you're in the middle of that, being filmed is the last thing on your mind. Now, hanging on this other line, I remembered what I had done yesterday. I started kicking the GoPro to try and wedge it back into a new position and clear it.

'Great thinking!' shouted Bear.

I wasn't thinking at all. It was all I had left in me,

strength-wise, to try and get myself out of the situation. Suddenly, it became clear that I was on the home straight as I inched towards the opposite cliff. I didn't know how long in real time I'd been dangling off the rope, but eventually I felt two arms swoop me up and pull me on to solid ground.

I tried to stand up, but through sheer adrenaline and exhaustion I couldn't. Bear was right in my face, giving me a hug.

'Extraordinary effort from you,' he said, with his typical enthusiasm. 'In all my years doing shows like this, and this particular challenge, no one has ever been able to do what you did today. Be proud of yourself, Alex. Rest up, you're going to need to get some of that strength back because it doesn't end here. It's just the beginning.'

I sat on the side of the cliff, waiting for the other contestants to complete the challenge, still shaking with fear as I was still thousands of feet in the sky. 'I'm not sure if I can do this,' I thought. 'It's too hard.'

Well. Despite my weak swimming ability and being terrified of heights, I won *Bear Grylls: Mission Survive*. It was so much more than a reality survival show for me. Every night we had to take it in turns to keep the fire alight to ward off animals. During these shifts, I would sit and just think about my life. I remember the stars shining so brightly above me and the magic of that – me, in complete darkness except for the glint of the stars and the flickering of the fire. It was then I would plug into my inner voice, which was telling me 'It's time to take the next step'. I had no idea what that step would look like but I knew what it meant: the time to leave football for good was coming up sooner rather than later.

Still, I was in total shock when I won the show. Not for one day during those two weeks did I think it was a possibility. I'd actually thought Sam would clinch it – she seemed to get through every task with flying colours and took everything on the chin. In the end, I didn't win because I was the best but because I played for the team. After the winner was announced, I stood in total shock (and tears), waiting for a helicopter that would whisk us off for the final bit of filming. Bear asked me why I was crying and I told him honestly, 'This doesn't happen to people like me, where I'm from, this isn't my world.'

He smiled at me then and told me that I both belonged here and to believe it, explaining why he'd picked me as the winner.

'I know that no matter the situation, out of everyone you would be the person to never leave me behind,' Bear told me. 'You'd be the person doing all you can to get everyone across the finish line – that's who I always want on my side.'

There was one moment that had decided it, Bear said. We'd been in a race against the clock to get back to base camp but Michelle Collins (who I'd grown up watching on TV in *EastEnders*) was really struggling at the back. Something inside me said, 'I don't care if I get booted off this show, I'm not going to leave someone in pain to struggle on their own.' So I carried Michelle's backpack and my own to ease up her load and told her no matter what, we'd make it to the finish line together. Bear saw what was happening and said he'd tried to test me, telling me at the time that I was putting my place at risk and to think long and hard about what I was doing. But I had! I thought Michelle was amazing on that show, even though she got in lots of arguments with the other celebs. All I saw was someone like my mum, a person stepping out of their comfort zone, trying to push through despite the pain.

When we got back to the hotel the first call I made (after a much-needed shower) was to Mum.

'Mum, it's me,' I said. She started screaming immediately, 'IT'S MY BABY!' She'd had no clue what we were going through as contact was banned. I could hear her crying down the phone and then heard her say to someone in the background, 'I'm so sorry, it's my daughter.'

'Mum, where are you?' I asked her, laughing. Turns out she was in Asda, doing the weekly shop. I promised to ring her back later, then paused.

'Wait, Mum, you didn't ask how I did?'

'I forgot it was a show!' she laughed. 'Well, you can't have bloody won, as you wouldn't be calling me!'

When I told her that, actually, I *had* won, the screaming started again. Sorry to the cashiers in Asda!

I pulled myself together and looked in the mirror; I was gaunt and all bone because I'd lost so much weight. Despite this, I was determined to join the wrap party – I had to, as the winner. Making my way downstairs, I looked for Sam. I was drooling at the thought of actual food, too – no more skinning a rat for dinner or trying to survive off the scraps we foraged along the way. I went straight for a burger and was handed a glass of champagne. One bite into my burger and half a glass of champagne down, I was feeling full and tipsy. My body couldn't handle the adjustment that quickly. Sam looked at me and whispered, 'Shall we just go to bed?'

'Yeah, let's sneak out,' I replied.

Just like that, thirty minutes into my 'winner's celebration' wrap party, I was tucked up in bed, fast asleep, with a smile on my face thinking about how I'd have to keep this amazing secret from everyone until the show aired.

9

Strength Is . . .
Knowing When To Take
The Next Step

Bear Grylls was filmed during a life-changing transitional period for me. I'd come back from participating in my third World Cup in Canada, having gone in as the starting right back. I left the tournament knowing the peak of my England career had been and gone. Once again, life followed a funny pattern: my first ever World Cup in an England shirt was also held in Canada, at U19s youth level. My last saw us knocked out in the semi-finals in the cruellest of ways, losing to Japan in the dying minutes of the game, with Laura Bassett scoring an own goal just as the referee was about to blow the whistle to take us into extra time. It was total heartbreak.

As is standard for summer tournaments, it was a baking hot day. I was a sub cheering the team on from the bench. When you're a sub, you tend to drink a lot more fluids and have to head off to the toilet more as a result – especially as you're constantly telling yourself, 'What if I go on the pitch and need the loo?' I'd just zoomed off on one of these trips and sat down to have a wee when mid-flow there was a BANG! and I heard the door to the changing room fly open.

'ALEX! ALEX! You're needed to play!' It was my teammate, Lianne Sanderson.

Having been pranked so many times over the years, I thought this was just another wind-up.

'Yeah, yeah,' I laughed, still on the toilet.

'Alex, for real, Lucy is throwing up on the pitch and is dizzy. You have to go on!'

I could tell now that Lianne was being serious. Within seconds, I was off the toilet seat, stripping off my gear and entering into a World Cup semi-final game without having even warmed up. My legs felt like lead and I was entering a fast-paced game, trying to get up to speed. Before I knew it, our World Cup Final dream was over. We did come home with a bronze medal and once again elevated women's football to another level and a bigger audience than ever before, however it was the start of goodbye for me. It had been over ten glorious years being known as the best right back in England and the world, but now a young Lucy Bronze announced herself to the world in the most spectacular of ways in that tournament, going on to become England's starting right back to the present day. And just as Heather Mitts had done for me when I was at Boston Breakers, I did all I could to support Lucy, challenging her and pushing her so when she eventually took my spot, she knew I'd be her biggest cheerleader – bar her mum, Diane (personally, I think I'm still up there though!).

Mine and Lucy's relationship is one I still treasure. We got on from day one. Even though we were in direct competition with each other, there was always this utmost respect between us. I would tell her what she needed to work on in regards to her game, and she would listen. We would sit and talk about almost anything in the world – she even helped me with my media degree, looking over my essays and editing them for me. I remember joking with her during the World Cup that I had twelve England goals – a lot for a right back – and if she wanted to be better than me, she would have to start shooting at the goal. We laughed.

'In all seriousness, Lucy, you get in great positions,' I added. 'Don't think about it, just shoot.'

Turns out Lucy really did listen to me because she went on to score a screamer of a goal in the next game England played in that tournament, the World Cup quarter-final against Norway. It cemented her as the best right back in the world. She later went on to be crowned as the best player in the world, full stop, at the Best FIFA Football Awards, the ultimate accolade a footballer can receive.

It would have been the easy option to step away from the national team immediately after the 2015 World Cup. But it didn't feel like the right time; I had no gut instinct to do so. Then-England manager Mark Sampson and the team staff had told me I still had a huge role to play in the team and how influential it was to have me around. I knew I was still good enough to be playing, but had to accept that Lucy was now ahead of me, so my game time would be different. I viewed playing for England in cycles: you have the Euros, then the World Cup, then the Olympics. As soon as one cycle ends, the qualification for another begins. I knew I had one more left in me and that would be the 2017 Euros, hosted by the Netherlands.

So I continued to put in the hard work to be at the top of my game. I had a leadership role and wanted to do all I could to support the other players. I believed after clinching the bronze medal at the 2015 World Cup, we could finally get a gold.

Today, I feel really lucky that I had something other than football to focus on during this period. My burgeoning broadcast career gave me a new passion and focus when I was training at the England camps. It also meant I missed a lot of the negativity that was brewing in the national squad, details of which would later emerge in the form of racism allegations. Eniola Aluko accused Mark and his staff of making racist jokes, and the FA of paying her what the *Guardian* called 'hush money' to 'avoid disruption' ahead of the 2017 Euros.

I feel guilty to say this all passed me by at the time, especially as another Black woman in the team. But maybe that speaks to how acclimatised to a certain culture we were as England footballers. And I just wasn't around as much; now I had another passion, I spent only a fraction of my time socialising, analysing team politics, or following the reasons given for why certain players were starting over others (especially as I was no longer the starting right back). When at England camps, I would train, go to team meetings, have dinner and then head to my room to work on media bits or watch a box set. Kaz Carney even commented on how 'different' I was to the Alex of years gone by. I always protested I wasn't different, I just had another career I was working on outside of football, but really, that in itself was a huge change. Football didn't consume every aspect of me anymore. I felt like there were other worlds to explore. So much so that the night before our opening game in the 2015 Canada World Cup, I was sitting in the hotel lobby finishing off my degree dissertation. As I pressed send on the submission email, I sat back and smiled to myself, thinking of young Alex. She'd struggled so much with education and now I'd just completed a university degree alongside my professional football career. I felt a little more confident that I could apply for a job after football in the media world and cite my degree on my CV.

Sometimes my new and old interests did overlap. In 2016, FIFA approached me, asking if I could lend a hand on an important project they were involved with in Papua New Guinea. They'd seen the work I'd done in Iraq with Arsenal (more on that to come) and wanted me on board to help women who had suffered, and still were suffering, from domestic violence and sexual harassment. Some of the young girls they were going to work with had been raped on the way to school. FIFA were planning to hold the 2016 U20s Women's World

Cup in Papua New Guinea, as part of a wider drive to change perceptions of women in ten Pacific nations. Within that region, 80 per cent of children had reportedly experienced some form of abuse.

Funny; until this book I've not spoken about domestic violence, but any projects brought to my attention along these lines, or that involve working with children, I am the first to say yes to. I find it incredible that simply through football or being on TV, I have the opportunity to help out others with issues I've personally gone through. I know first-hand that the most important thing to give sometimes is a bit of joy and hope. So wherever it was possible to make these commitments work around my football playing schedule, I would. It would be selfish of me to say no just because I might miss a couple of hours' sleep.

I told FIFA I had a four-day window between an Arsenal game and meeting up with the England team. FIFA looked at every which way to make it work so I could get over to Papua New Guinea and be able to go into the schools, give talks and actually be present in the local communities. We managed to sort something out – the only slight snag would be the time I arrived at the England camp in the Netherlands for our last friendly of the 2016 calendar.

In my head, this plan worked out fine for all parties. I wasn't skipping any Arsenal training and I wouldn't miss any sessions with England either. The only thing it meant was not sitting with the other girls on the plane.

I'd arrive in the Netherlands on the same night and be ready for training the next day. I spoke with Mark Sampson and he agreed on the plan. Great. Off I went to the other side of the world. Having already travelled a bit, I had an expectation of the kind of work I would be doing and what I might see. I had tried to do some reading about PNG, and the articles I did find painted a very gloomy picture: lots of reports about kidnaps, rapes and cannibals. I thought PNG would be grey, dirty and dull to be honest. How wrong I was! The first morning, I discovered a paradise, bright sunshine and lush greenery everywhere. I was met with joy and smiles from everyone I came into contact with. First on the agenda was joining a march. Thousands had taken to the streets to protest against domestic violence. Word had spread that I was there – I had little kids running up to me, trying to shake my hand and walk with me. One of my favourite photos from that trip is of this girl, reaching out to shake my hand – the smile on her face is everything.

Later that day, I went to see the Papua New Guinea U20s team playing in their first ever World Cup match. A few years earlier, the squad hadn't even existed. By seventy minutes, the team were 6-0 down, but then something magical happened. Not only had 20,000 people turned up to cheer the women's side on, but the team then scored their first – and only – goal of the tournament. The stadium erupted. I kid you not, tears of joy were running down the faces of everyone present and the impact the next day was huge. No one cared that the girls had ultimately lost the game 6-1. They were seen as local heroes and role models for representing their country with pride. I spent the whole of the next day going into schools with the team to give talks to packed assembly halls. At the first school, I tried to get the girls to speak but they were too shy. Instead I had them stand beside me, front and centre, as I told stories, trying to make them laugh. By the time we reached our third destination, their confidence was up and they stood on stage, recalling their lives and telling the assembled audience about what sport had done for them as young women. It was absolutely magic to watch them literally grow through the day, feeding off the energy of the people who were looking up to them as inspirations. It was one of those trips that will stay with me until my last breath, a reminder of just how much the power of sport can be used to create change. I left Papua New Guinea feeling on top of the world about what had been achieved, and buzzing to meet up with the England team as a result. I wanted to end the international year on a high.

I made it to the Netherlands as planned and was there bright and early for our first team training the next day; it was freezing cold. Mark was absent – his wife was due to give birth so he was flying over that evening. When he did arrive, he requested a meeting with me. I turned up as asked, confused as to what he could want to discuss.

'Als,' Mark told me, looking serious, 'I'm disappointed. You were going to start this game but I can't play you now. You've been off around the world doing "stuff". You didn't meet up with the team as normal. I dunno. I can't play you.'

I stared at him, gobsmacked. None of what Mark was saying made sense. Firstly, I wasn't a starting player anymore, full stop. Lucy Bronze was. Why would that change? Secondly, he was talking like he was going to do me a favour by starting me. No thanks. I earned every single one of my 140 England caps. I didn't need pity or favours. Thirdly, Mark had signed off on the plan, so what was all this? I hadn't missed a single training session. The only one of us who had was Mark himself.

I've never felt rage and frustration erupt in my body the way it did that evening, sitting on a sofa with Mark in the Netherlands. He carried on talking but I couldn't hear it. A red mist had descended. All I could think about was being in Papua New Guinea a day earlier, where women endured so much and young girls couldn't even get to school safely. I'd seen what mattered, the positive impact football could have, and now I had to sit here and listen to petty team politics. At that moment, I felt something snap.

A tear ran down my face. I looked at Mark and he stopped talking. 'What's up, Als?' he said.

'Mark,' I replied, my voice shaking with anger. 'I quit! I don't want to play for England anymore. I'm done. This will be my last camp and then I'm done for good.'

Mark stared at me, pure panic written across his face.

'What do you mean?'

'I'm done, Mark, I've had enough. I don't *want* you to pick me anymore. I'm retiring.'

I remember his reaction: utter shock. I'd clearly said the last thing he would have expected. Fair enough, as I'd had zero idea those words were going to come out of my mouth either. If I hadn't just come from Papua New Guinea, maybe things would have gone differently. But my purpose had been reframed over the last year from playing football to being able to help people through football in a different way. No longer was being *on* the pitch my ultimate goal.

I got up from the sofa. 'Mark, thank you for your time, but I'm done.'

Kaz looked alarmed when I came into our shared room, tears streaming down my face.

'Reens, are you OK?' she asked.

'I've just quit, Kaz,' I told her. 'I can't do this anymore. I can't go on like this.'

Kaz detected I'd exploded in a way that was unusual for me and advised me to take some time to think about it. We were talking it through when I saw I had three missed calls from Mum. I paused my conversation with Kaz to call her back.

'Mum, are you OK? Sorry, I had a meeting, I missed your calls.'

'Alex,' she said, her voice tight with excitement. 'You have a letter!'

My first thought was annoyance – why were people

still sending my post to my mum's address? I sighed and told her I'd grab it off her next week.

'Al, it looks important! Shall I open it?'

I felt so exhausted, tear tracks still down my face from having quit my international career in such a dramatic fashion.

'OK, Mum, open it, let me know what it says.'

There was a minute during which I could hear her prising open the envelope and skimming its contents. Then she started screaming.

'ALEX, IT'S FROM THE QUEEN! YOU'VE BEEN AWARDED AN MBE!'

More screaming! The tears started up again on my side as I realised the enormity of what she was saying. There was some laughter too; I'd just found out I'd been awarded an MBE for services to women's football minutes after I'd told my international manager I'd quit. You couldn't make it up.

After that camp, Mark and a number of the coaching staff did their best to get me to change my mind. I can be very stubborn (as if you haven't clocked that yet!). If it wasn't for a chat with Marieanne Spacey, I probably would have ended my career right there and then. But she made me understand why I needed to see it through to the Euros and go out with (hopefully) a gold medal.

We didn't leave the 2017 Euros with gold. To be honest, we weren't tactically the best in that tournament and were found out in the semi-final. I remember sitting on the bench, post-game, when everyone had gone in, thinking, 'This is it . . . international career, done.' Of all the people that could have consoled me, it was my team-mate, friend and the woman who has gone on to be the best player in the world who came and put her arm around me. Lucy and I said nothing but we both cried. It was the end of an era – for me, anyway.

Even though I'd retired from England, I wasn't done with Arsenal yet. It has always been my home and I knew I wanted to go back there to continue to play.

I was so used to winning trophies with Arsenal. My entire career had been one of successive silver-ware: league titles, FA Cups, Champions League. With Arsenal, I had won every domestic honour the game had to offer, multiple times, and the feeling never got old for me. Yet, despite those wins, I could feel frustration bubbling up, frustration that had been brewing for several years before my England retirement.

Women's football was not progressing the way it deserved to. Even at one of the biggest clubs in the country, we were being treated like constant after-thoughts, all while we were pretending to the outside world that Arsenal was setting standards and leading the way. The sad thing was, Arsenal had initially done that; it had taken a huge amount of work just to get standards increased from 'non-existent' to 'bottom tier'. But now other clubs like Manchester City had professionalised and overtaken us. When Manchester City Women came into the WSL they entered with a bang, big statements and investment, declaring they would set the standard and take women's football to the next level in this country. They signed Steph Houghton as captain and wanted to sign me too. I had a meeting with them to discuss the offer; what they were proposing blew me away, to be honest. The club was going to be streets ahead of Arsenal in terms of facilities afforded, and the model they had put in place was closer to what it had felt like playing pro in America. And not only had Man City spied an opportunity, but Chelsea, with Emma Hayes as manager, were starting to build as well. As a club, Arsenal had stood still, and it showed. But none of it was quite enough to tempt me away. My heart has always been with Arsenal and everyone bloody knows it. It says so much about my love and loyalty to the club that I turned down Manchester City. They were going to pay me more than I was ever offered at Arsenal my whole life, but when I weighed it all up – having been at Arsenal since I was eight, my life in London, my degree – it meant more to me than the extra money I would get at City. But I did let Arsenal know how close they were to losing me that season, and how sad I was that it felt like other clubs valued me more than Arsenal did.

My frustrations still leaked through to the outside world though. Perhaps one of the most telling incidents was when I was asked by the *Guardian* to give an interview in 2015, as part of a big piece intended to shine a positive light on women's football and, in particular, Arsenal. I told Clare Wheatley the paper had been in touch and asked her if we could set up ten minutes before training to sit and chat to the journalist in the area dedicated to us on those evenings. No, came the response. The club won't allow it. A journalist in the training ground? No such thing. I tried to explain that the paper was basically doing us a favour, giving us the coverage we weren't getting and desperately needed. Plus, journalists were at the training ground all the time – for the men.

No dice.

I felt so embarrassed. Here I was, Arsenal captain, having to organise an interview about my club at a Starbucks around the corner. The journalist might have caught *me* on a bad day, but it turned into a good one for them as my venting quickly gave them a bigger story than expected. I told them straight, that I was just as embarrassed as they were that I was sitting in Starbucks in my full training gear, having to wait for the men to leave the ground before we were even allowed in. That it was a joke, a complete joke. I wasn't really thinking; I was annoyed. I don't know what was going on behind the scenes, but from where I was sitting it felt like Arsenal was internally begging for more media coverage but externally not trying to make it happen – it was someone else's job to take care of. Days later, I was about to go on air for the *Women's Football Show* when my phone blinked with a text from Casey Stoney.

'Well done for speaking up,' it read.

Confused, I replied, asking what she was talking about. Casey's next message was screenshots of the *Guardian* piece. There, in black and white, were all my frustrations.

I was shitting myself. Who was I to speak out against my club or make the public think anything but great things about Arsenal? Obviously management at the club saw it and it didn't reflect well at all. I apologised. It's funny though; next season, there was a restructure. And suddenly we were allowed our own space at the training ground, we had morning training like any other professional footballers, and lunch was now offered at the ground, so players could focus on nutrition if they weren't already doing so. Despite these steps forward, for the first time I could sense the end of my time at Arsenal drawing near. We were in such a transitional stage at the club, and a particularly difficult one. It wasn't the most positive of environments, as most periods of change tend to be. Many players were unhappy, the old guard were retiring, and we had a manager who clashed with a lot of the team. As captain, I felt in the middle of it all and was shouldering a lot of responsibility to try and fix things, as well as being the sounding board for player frustrations. This is all part of the gig – but I was getting home most nights mentally and physically drained. Having already stepped away from the England team, I recognised the signs: I was done.

I still managed to rack up one more incredible moment as part of the team though. When people ask me now what my favourite memory of my footballing career is, I say the same thing. Everyone expects me to pick the 2007 Champions League win, where I scored the winning goal. But for me, it was clinching the 2016 FA Cup trophy, with a Wembley final. I'd always dreamed of playing there, ever since I was first plucked from the football cages of east London, and I'd done so at the Olympics, but now there I was with my family of twenty-three years. The sun was glorious that day. We were the underdogs, up against Emma Hayes' Chelsea. But from the warm-up we knew we were going to win. It's a feeling you cannot explain; something a bit like fate. And win we did. I remember walking up the Wembley stairs, crying like a baby. And a voice in my head saying, 'Alex, you've had one last special moment playing with the team – this is it. Savour it.'

As captain, I'd already taken it upon myself to ensure that whatever happened in the match, people remembered the day. So the victorious Arsenal Ladies returned triumphant to one of the biggest parties we ever had as a team. I'd cut a deal with a cool venue in London, organised a DJ, food, a guest list for friends and family – the lot. Amazingly, I'd even managed to sweet talk Clare into getting the top brass to give us £2,000, and then each player contributed £40 of their own cash. On top of that, I used £1,500 of my own money to cover the rest of the costs to make sure we had the best time. My teammate Emma Mitchell always used to get mad at me when I did things like that, because then I'd be out of pocket, but I loved seeing people enjoy these moments. Yes, I was £1,500 short on my mortgage that month, but this time the debt man wasn't knocking at my door, and to this day, everyone still remembers that party!

For me, that really was a last hurrah. After the Cup

Final, tensions worsened. In 2016, representatives from the Arsenal men's team arranged a meeting with me and the charity Save the Children. It turned out Save the Children and Arsenal Foundation were planning a trip and they wanted me and a male player to lead it. We'd be heading to Iraq, through a danger zone, to visit children at one of the refugee camps to open a football cage for them. I said yes straight away. The club told me they'd sort everything with the women's department and schedule the trip around my training so I wouldn't miss anything. But it wasn't that simple; the disconnect between the Arsenal the male players experienced and the Arsenal the women played for soon showed up. My then-manager, Pedro Losa, called me into his office and told me point blank: 'Alex, you're not going.'

He said I would have to tell the club – the club he worked for – no.

'It's not good, on your off days you should be completely resting,' he reasoned. 'And what will the other players think if I allow this?' Truth be told, I was furious. I tried to be respectful but firm, and told my manager strongly that *he* would be the one to pass this decision on to the club. I wasn't the one letting my club down over a fear of what another player would think about what I was choosing to do on my two days off. I went home that day seething. The trip was so much bigger than football to me – it was giving these kids some hope and a chance to actually be children, amid the chaos of war. The more I thought about it, the more determined I became. I knew how it felt to be trapped and for a football cage to present one of the only bright spots of daily life. I couldn't just sit on my sofa on *my own* day off. So the next day I went and told my manager – who was shocked at my sudden assertiveness – that next week I'd agreed to go to Iraq. I was off. In the event of it, I was the only footballer on the trip. My male counterpart had pulled out – he was too scared about the potential dangers. But I focused on the job in hand. When we got to the camp, I was taken straight to the football cage that had been built with funds from the Arsenal Foundation. I had not felt the pure happiness I got from being with those kids for a long time. We played football for an hour and then did a Q&A, but mainly I listened to their stories; these little voices piping up, telling me they wanted to be doctors and nurses so they could 'save people', but also be footballers because it made them feel 'free'. Every so often a child would sprint off and return, clutching flowers that they would thrust towards me. It was so beautiful being around them.

I don't want to gloss over the hardship though. After visiting the cage, I was taken to the home of a young girl who'd been playing with us. I tried not to cry; I didn't want her to think I felt sorry for her. She was sleeping on the floor of a single room with ten other family members and I felt so helpless, so unable to do anything, that I broke. She took my hand and told me that it was OK, that I didn't need to cry and that my visit had given her the strength to know that good things were going to happen to her. It sounds like something out of a movie, but I promise you it happened – and as you can imagine, I cried even more.

For safety reasons, and because of the agreement negotiated with Arsenal, I had to leave Iraq the same day I arrived. I walked out of the camp with a new perspective on life – and on football. Someone who materially had nothing wanted to give me all she had that day, and just me being there as an Arsenal women's footballer was enough to give her a bit of light. That felt magical. I realised I had a new purpose to what I was doing, and could do, with my platform. I wanted to harness that feeling I'd had in Iraq again and knew I could no longer find that on the pitch. Upon seeing the positive media reaction, my manager apologised to me when I returned. He said he hadn't realised exactly what I was being asked to do. I thanked him but I didn't really need an apology; the trip hadn't been for my benefit.

With my future and retirement from Arsenal Ladies now decided, Christmas 2017 rolled around. I spent the lead-up packing, preparing to move house. In the process I discovered the stacks and stacks of football boots and spare kit I'd received from thirteen years of Puma sponsorship. So I fired off a tweet saying if anyone wanted boots or kit, let me know and I'd come drop it off in my car. A reply from an account called Football Beyond Borders caught my eye; I did a quick google and discovered they were a social inclusion charity, helping kids who love football but are disengaged at school to achieve both on and off the pitch. Well . . . that was a story I was all too familiar with! I knew I had to get involved. So on Christmas Eve I packed the car full of Puma kit, my England and Arsenal jerseys and picked up my niece. We rocked up to a slightly run-down shop on a council estate that had been converted into a hangout spot for the kids helped by the organisation, and spent the day making friends, eating a Christmas dinner and hearing all their stories. I left thinking I had to do some-thing more for them. They were all mad about Arsenal and football in general, but because of their circum-stances and the astronomical price of tickets, none of these kids had ever been to a Premier League match, or even to a football ground. All they had was the football cage in the estate, like I had growing up.

Suddenly it clicked – I had done some work with Arsenal, the wider club, a couple of months prior and had felt bad when they mentioned paying me ('Why?' I wonder now). Instead I'd told them that for one men's game, I'd like to have a box to watch the match with my family and friends and that was all the payment needed. They'd agreed – and I still had the box to use. Now, in a lightbulb moment, I realised that I could take these kids to an Arsenal game, and not just in a standard seat – they were going to live it up! When I say that day was one of my favourites, it barely covers it. It was so, so special. I told the club what I wanted to do, and they couldn't have been more helpful at making those kids' dreams come true. Fifteen of them came down in the end; I took them pitch-side and, I won't lie, there were some tears – of joy, I hope! We watched the players get off the team bus and after the game I'd arranged for Alex Iwobi to come up, which he did, talking to all the kids and taking photos with them. That's when it was my turn for tears; it made me cry seeing how much it meant to them. It was a day of laughter too, though – especially when the kids told me they'd never tasted burgers like the ones at the Emirates and they would never forget the food alongside the football!

That night shored up my belief that I could now have a bigger impact off the pitch than on it.

The way I retired from Arsenal had a lot of similarities with how I bowed out from England – I had a gut feeling and it kind of came out of the blue. Or so I thought. At the time, these things feel like surprises, but laying it out on the page makes the path to retirement look a lot more linear. I didn't think long and hard about leaving. I knew if I did, I'd talk myself out of it. In October 2017 Pedro Losa had his contract terminated by the club, now the freshly rebranded 'Arsenal Women'. I spoke to Clare Wheatley about a new manager coming in and went to a hotel to meet a candidate by the name of Joe Montemurro. Straight away, I could see Joe had the energy and passion the club had been lacking for a while. I left the meeting feeling a weight had been lifted off my shoulders. Clare and I both had a notion that Joe was the man for the job – and it turned out he was. The feeling of relief I had that day, leaving the meeting with

Joe, was that I was ready to hand everything over to him. I was officially done. I didn't need to carry the weight of the team anymore. I had so much love for Arsenal that I'd taken on these extra duties to try and make the club the best possible. But I didn't have to anymore.

The following week, Joe's appointment had yet to be announced but I was off to an awards show for women in sport, as a representative of Arsenal. The event organisers had asked if I would be OK to take a couple of questions from the press, so I agreed. It had been a month since my international retirement had been officially announced and the first question I received, naturally, was centred on how I felt about that. The second, from Jeanette Kwakye, threw me off guard.

'So, Alex, how much longer do you think you will play on?' she asked.

I looked at her, giggled, and said: 'Well, this is the first time I am saying this, but this is going to be my final season with Arsenal.'

You could hear a pin drop. I could tell everyone was thinking: 'Did she just mean to say that?' To be honest, I'm not even sure I did, but just like that I'd announced my retirement from football, off the cuff. What I didn't know was that these awards were being live-streamed via the Sky Sports YouTube channel. Within minutes, Sky Sports and the BBC were running headlines that 'Alex Scott announces this will be her final season with Arsenal'. As I sat back down in my chair, my phone began pinging with messages. Clare was trying to ring me but I wasn't ready to take calls. I didn't even know what to say. A text from her flashed up on screen: 'Thanks for the heads-up with that one'. Thing is, I didn't have a heads-up myself. I was just as shocked that I'd finally spoken the words out loud and now there was no going back. At training the next day, the team were just as surprised but very supportive. Clare said she was disappointed the club had had no time to plan a big announcement or put the news out first. Maybe it was the best way though; I didn't need a big announcement. I had a couple of months to see out the end of the season so I wasn't going anywhere yet.

Joe came in as manager and straight away, it was great. His arrival made the process of me stepping aside much easier, with other players now able to take on leadership roles in the team. I joke that if Joe had come in a year earlier, maybe I *would* have signed that new contract I was in discussions about. But I know deep down I couldn't. Signing a two-year deal at that point would have been taking the safe option.

Announcing my retirement was a HUGE gamble. I didn't have any regular TV work lined up and there was no guarantee I'd be getting any more gigs than the sporadic ones I was already doing. But I've always been more of the mindset that thinks 'what if this does work out?' rather than 'what if it doesn't?'. And so far, that's gone pretty well. My club and the fans gave me a fairy-tale ending to my nearly thirty-year career on the pitch. Thank you to all the fans at my last league game at

Borehamwood, who saw me out singing 'We love you, Scottie, we do', and to the 60,000 fans at the Emirates who bellowed 'She's one of our own' when I was paraded on to the pitch after the last men's game of the season. I cried at the reception and felt so loved and appreciated for what I had achieved for my club.

Also hilarious was when the Arsenal fans made up a new song for me which went, 'She's won more than you, she's won more than you, Tottenham Hotspur, she's won more than you'. Facts only!

I don't think I'll ever be able to articulate how much Arsenal has given me throughout my life. To Arsenal FC: you gave a little girl hope, you gave me an escape, you gave me a chance. Arsenal is me yesterday, today and tomorrow. Always. THANK YOU.

10

Strength Is . . .
Celebrating Wins

I'm absolutely rubbish at celebrating 'wins' for myself. Birthdays, dinners, award shows . . . doesn't matter – I'm always so focused on making sure everyone else has a great time, I forget to make sure I'm actually enjoying myself. Prime example was my birthday in October 2021. I was coming off an amazing professional year, I've got this team around me who are more than just colleagues, they're friends – my hairdresser, my stylist, all these people – so I thought, 'You know what, we're going to have a celebration, my way of saying thanks.' I incorporated it with my birthday and paid for everyone. For real, I don't think I've ever spent that much money in one night. It was 100 per cent worth it, but I was so stressed about everyone else having a good time that I didn't stop and take a moment to try and let the achievements I was supposed to be celebrating actually sink in.

I've realised that the 'wins' for me, the bits that make me feel alive and blessed, are not the big glitzy occasions. The times I feel at my happiest or when I really recognise just how much I've achieved, are the quiet moments. Like when I've finished my morning run and there's this amazing sunrise. That sounds so cheesy but it's true. Or being in beautiful blue water, diving, thinking, 'I can't believe I'm doing this.' Standing on top of a hill after a hike and marvelling at the fact that I have found myself there right in that second. These quiet, still stretches are when I celebrate the wins, of just being there in the first place. These are the wow moments.

I don't want to pretend that the glitzy occasions can't be fun though. And I've got great stories. Like my first *GQ* Men of the Year Awards in 2018. These are big, fancy occasions where you come across notable people from so many different walks of life – you can find yourself next to anyone, from Sacha Baron Cohen to Prince Charles. I was presenting an award to Harry Kane that evening and was properly nervous.

Stepping into the world of fashion was a totally new thing for me. I'd gone out earlier to buy a dress and been talked into getting something ridiculously expensive on someone else's recommendation. I didn't have the kind of money to spend on a piece of clothing I would only ever wear once, but at the same time I knew I needed a 'nice' dress. What I ended up with was not me at all: bright pink and too long. Experimenting with style and fashion is something I've grown to love in the years since, but that first shopping excursion . . . what a bust. I did get to borrow some really fancy diamonds though, that were so expensive I spent the whole night checking the rings and necklace were still on me. If I'd lost them, I'd have been in debt for the rest of my life (that debt man I've been so scared of would have finally got me!). The panic was real but it was worth it; it was my *Pretty Woman* moment. When Julia Roberts' character puts on that diamond necklace, you can tell she instantly feels expensive. Those diamonds gave me a little something too. What I've learned since the first *GQ* Awards I attended is that, no matter what, I still need to feel like 'me' in whatever it is that I'm wearing. That first dress made me feel like I was trying to be something I wasn't, truth be told. I'm never going to allow myself to do that again.

The awards were the very next day after the shopping trip. Suddenly I found myself pulling up to the venue, getting out of the car and being ushered to the red carpet. I was in front of what looked like millions of photographers all snapping away: pap, pap, pap! The way they shouted was overwhelming. I'm thinking: 'Oh my gosh, I shouldn't even be here.' I had no clue how to walk down a red carpet; I could only just about walk at all in my dress and heels. No one had ever taught me how to pose. How do you even prepare for that? But then it was my turn. I'd nearly built up the courage to go when: 'Wait, wait, wait, hold the carpet!' A group of big burly bodyguards pushed through and all of a sudden there's Kate Beckinsale being chaperoned in front of me, walking the carpet. She was a pro – Pow! Pow! Pow! – working every single angle possible. I must have turned white. My mind was racing, thinking, 'How the *heck* do I follow that? I can't even walk in heels. I feel so embarrassed for myself already.' For real, at that moment I wanted the ground to open up and swallow me whole.

Then there was a tap on my shoulder.

I turned around. It was Zendaya. You know. *Zendaya.*

'Don't worry,' she said, with a kind smile. 'You'll be fine.'

'Thanks!' I squeaked, and shuffled my way down the carpet. I don't think she knew how much the gesture meant at that moment. This was my first taste of how the celebrity scene operated – up until then I'd been in a sports bubble. Now here I was, seeing the likes of Donatella Versace walk past me, and I went right back to being that kid in my bedroom, who'd never have dreamed she'd be in a room with all these people. When Kate Beckinsale strode down that carpet, I'd honestly wanted to disappear – I thought it must be so obvious how awkward I felt.

But the stories I have from that night are so funny. Walking up on stage, presenting an award to Harry Kane . . . only it turned out he wasn't there, so I kept the award and walked off the stage. Then I was ushered to a room in the back and an interview with someone I now know well: Maya Jama. Her first question to me, on camera, was: 'Hi Alex, soooooooo, tell us who are you wearing?' The question threw me. I hadn't got a bloody clue. Now I know about all things fashion, but at those first awards I wasn't prepared in the slightest.

'I don't have a clue,' I told Maya. 'I was in a rush and bought it yesterday at Selfridges.'

She must have thought: 'Who let this chick in?' I mean, how embarrassing when you're at a fashion awards! I was so far out of my comfort zone. It's hilarious looking back now, as the *GQ* Awards has become one of my favourite events.

That night was also my first taste of an 'after-AFTER party'. How the hell I got invited to this thing, I will never know. But there I was, rocking up to a place that was chock-full of A-list stars. Me and my manager at the time, Jake, were trying to be all cool, while I was sticking out like a sore thumb in this pink dress I didn't even know the bloody designer of. Suddenly, I felt another tap on my shoulder.

'Hi,' said this tall, Black American man.

'Hi, I'm Alex,' I said. 'Alex Scott.' Not a clue why I full-named myself. There were those nerves again.

'Yes, I know who you are.' I nearly fell over, because I knew exactly who he was too – *Black Panther* had been a global phenomenon and he was the lead.

'You played soccer in America, right?' Chadwick Boseman continued.

'Yes, I played for Boston,' I said, keeping it together. We chatted a little while about football and how much I'd loved living in America, until I excused myself from the conversation, worried Jake (my agent at the time) would be on his own. Afterwards I couldn't believe it – Chadwick Boseman knew who I was! Another one of those moments where I had to ask myself 'Did that really happen to me? Alex from Poplar?'

I had to leave the party 'early' at 3am. People couldn't believe I was heading out, as things were still in full swing as I said my goodbyes. But I was on a flight to Rwanda at 8am to represent Arsenal Football Club, which included naming a baby gorilla in front of 60,000 people. Another one of those Alex Scott 'pinch yourself' moments.

Aside from feeling out of place at glamorous awards shows, there are obvious reasons why I find it hard to 'celebrate' in the traditional way. It's the survival mentality – always having to move on to the next achievement. If I stop, I'm scared that everything I've worked for will melt away and I'll end up right back on the council estate. That's always been one of my biggest fears, which makes me feel so guilty. It's not because of the stigma of the estate – as I've discussed, I'm so proud of where I come from. It's the memories. But still, it adds up, so the actual moment of a 'win' is difficult to celebrate. It's in the aftermath that I can take stock, or even just while on the journey. I can't really process the weight of an occasion at the time, or without bringing my loved ones along – it's their pride and approval I'm really looking for. What's the point in 'winning' if I can't share it with the people I care about most? Like when I was awarded my MBE.

Going to the palace to pick up my award was one of the most special days of my life. Not many things will top that. The whole day was not about me (beyond the fact I was picking up the honour), but instead it's a memory I will treasure because I got to celebrate with the two most amazing women in my life: my mum and my nan. I wanted this to be their day. They'd got me to where I was. They were the women who had shaped me. So it had to be an occasion to remember. I emailed the Ritz personally and said, I'm off to the palace to get my MBE but please, would they be able to squeeze me in for afternoon tea with my family to celebrate? The Ritz emailed straight back: they would love to accommodate us. I was made up and kept everything under wraps. It was to be a surprise – the palace, then the Ritz! Imagine! Growing up, *Charlie and the Chocolate Factory* was one of my top two favourite films (the other was *Mary Poppins*, obviously). There was something so magical about Charlie getting that golden ticket and taking Grandpa Joe on this wonderful adventure. It's a fable about kindness. When I say I loved that film – I bloody *loved* it. Getting my MBE that day was a *Charlie and the Chocolate Factory* moment. I'd organised picking Mum and my niece, Skye, up, then it was off to Wapping to collect Nan, who hadn't been out much because illness was starting to get to her.

Mum and Nan were done up to the nines. We were dropped off at the palace gates; I showed my letter and off we went inside. Like Grandpa Joe, Nan had her walking stick and we had to proceed slowly, but we managed. The ceremony was quite long – as is my way, I was getting worried about Nan and Mum and if they had water. I knew Skye would be fine; I'd wanted her to come so she could see that if she set her mind to it, there were so many things she could achieve. If you're collecting something like an MBE, you're told in advance all the formalities you have to follow: what you have to do when your name is called, how not to turn your back on the royal presenting you with the award, and so on. But it's still nerve-racking. There's an entire room of eyes on you. I remember Princess Anne asking me why I'd retired from England, and saying the work I'd done off the pitch was of huge significance in helping women. To be honest, I can't even remember what I said in response, but once she shook my hand, I knew the conversation was done. I nearly gave myself a heart attack because in that moment I went to turn away before immediately remembering the number one rule: never turn your back on a royal. Instead, I stumbled backward, embarrassed and worried people may have clocked what I'd been about to do. Then, just like that, it was all over. I was reunited with Mum, Nan and Skye for official photos and then that part of the day was done.

I told Mum and Nan I'd sorted a taxi to get us home but we just needed to walk up through Green Park to get away from the traffic. I could see the Ritz in the distance and kept reassuring them that the taxi was just at the top of the road. When we got there, we walked a little further and then we were outside the Ritz.

'Surprise!' I said. 'Let's go in here.'

Mum's shock was all over her face.

'What, the Ritz?'

'Yes, Mum, we're going to the Ritz.'

I was beaming with pride, about to burst with the fact that I was treating them to a fancy afternoon to top off such a special day. We were ushered to our table and presented with a bottle of champagne as a congratulations for my MBE. We spent the rest of the afternoon in the Ritz, enjoying a lavish afternoon tea. It's precious hours I'll never forget: Nan smiling so happily, sipping champagne as she nodded her head to the music softly playing in the background. Mum couldn't believe she was in the Ritz and phoned my brother immediately to tell him where we were. Skye was suddenly faced with the difficult decision of which delicate little cake she was going to try next. My best friend Regan also came to join us, to complete the crew. Later, after I dropped Nan and Mum off, I sat on Mum's sofa for a bit before heading home myself.

'Mum, I know we may not have long left with Nan,' I said, after a while, 'but I will always remember her face from today.'

To this day, when I picture my nan, it's in the Ritz, nodding her head to the music and sipping champagne. I knew, right then, without any words needed, how proud she was of me. But I was proud in turn, that I'd been able to give Nan and Mum that special moment that honestly wasn't about me at all. It was a thank you to them. Success can be viewed in so many ways.

Personally, it's never been about the material things that only benefit me as an individual. The success I've managed to achieve in my life is crowned by the special moments it's given me with those I hold closest. That's the sort of win I celebrate.

11

Strength Is . . .
Asking For Help

The title of my book is very much a lesson I am still learning: how not to be strong. Up until the point I stepped into therapy, everything was about being outwardly invulnerable. Don't show emotion, be tough. If I was physically strong as well, I could deal with anything that came my way. The messages I was getting from society backed this up. Athletes should be strong. Black women *have* to be strong. Little girls from Poplar estates, fighting their corner, aren't given the room *not* to be strong. Everything came back to that one word, when actually I needed to learn the opposite: how to be soft, to be vulnerable, to be open to support.

I have never been able to ask for help. No matter how big or small the problem at hand, I've always had this voice in my head insisting that 'I can do it alone'. I'm laughing, recalling partners trying to lend a helping hand as I assemble furniture, and me, terrier-like, refusing to let them near the screwdriver – even if the instructions clearly stated it was a two-person job. From cooking to my mental health, for most of my life I just couldn't accept outside help. Until one evening, when thirty-odd years of going it alone finally stopped working.

The lowest point of my life started coming to a head on a day people usually spend looking forward to the future. It was 31 December 2018, New Year's Eve. My social media feeds were full of pictures of people celebrating with their loved ones and friends. My phone screen was choked with notifications of unanswered messages inviting me to do the same. But I didn't want to see a soul. Red wine was my only company that evening. I spent a few hours not really watching the TV, crying on and off. At the time I didn't understand the tears. I drank enough wine to fog my brain and send me to sleep, hoping I would wake up the next morning renewed.

I was kicking off 2019 with a double shift at Sky, which was great. I loved going to work. It felt like the one place where I was happy. Looking back, I was repeating the same patterns I had done earlier at the training ground – using work as a space to completely compartmentalise and repress whatever else was going on in my life. But on 1 January 2019, all I knew was the anticipation I felt of getting into the studio and shaking off the miasma that had been dogging me. That day I was paired up with Graeme Souness, with David Jones presenting. I really loved working with both of them. David would always give me the confidence to express my opinions, and knew no matter what subject we had to talk about, I would be ready and poised to answer. Graeme also challenged me in a way I hugely appreciated. After the show that day, he asked if he could have a quick word. My first thought was to fret; had I said something on air that had offended him? But no.

'I have to apologise to you,' Graeme started. 'When you first started working with us, I have to be honest, I wasn't sure. I didn't know much about you, what you could bring or even your understanding of the game.'

He confessed he was of a 'certain generation' and that he'd had some preconceptions of my abilities, but that now he saw he'd been wrong.

'You're a credit to the team and a lovely girl,' he finished. 'I just wanted to say that.'

To say I was absolutely buzzing was an understatement. To have Graeme say those words to me in that moment meant more than he could ever have known. I'd started to get a lot of trolling online, which only increased the more I appeared across Sky Sports platforms. I knew that to thousands of fans watching I didn't have the luxury of just representing myself as Alex Scott, former footballer; I was Alex Scott, a WOMAN in what they considered to be a man's world. It was a huge amount of pressure and responsibility but it was fine, I thought. 'I'm handling it on my own. It's all good.' I left the studio with the previous night's tears and low mood feeling a world away, reflecting on how lucky I was to be doing a job I absolutely loved and being acknowledged as a woman in this space.

But then I got home. The term I've since learned for

what I was going through is 'functioning depressive'. I loved my job so much that it was keeping me going, but in the aftermath I would return to a dark place.

I was in a new apartment which wasn't quite home yet, even though I loved the local area. WhatsApp messages from friends were pinging through to my phone but I ignored them, instead pouring myself a glass of wine and then a few more. I was struck by this great feeling of just wanting to be alone, maybe forever, and then I remember walking into my bedroom and past my mirror. I paused and went back a few paces until I was standing in front of my reflection, just staring. And then I collapsed. It was an eruption of emotion. I can still see myself now, like an out-of-body experience, gazing down at the other Alex, curled in a foetal position on the bed, her whole form heaving with sobs, the sort of crying where you can't even catch your breath. For weeks I'd been coming home, drinking to numb my emotions. It had worked on and off but now the dam had burst. What I'd seen when I looked in the mirror was a girl absolutely mired in sadness and loneliness, and it had all been too much. I just couldn't understand why I would be feeling like this; I had a dream job, great friends, a loving family. I had nothing to be sad about, yet despite that, here I was, in bits. I had everything and yet felt utterly empty.

That night was a wake-up call. For so long I had been just about surviving mentally – surviving was what I knew best. I cried myself to sleep but before I finally passed out, I told myself that I couldn't do it anymore. I needed help.

Waking up the next day, that was my one goal: to find help. I didn't want to keep turning to drink to numb my feelings – I'd seen the impact that had had on my loved ones. But equally, my lifelong method of just tamping down complex emotions was no longer working. There was no more space inside me to repress them. I had to confront them head on. I didn't really know anything about the different options available but my first thought was that I needed therapy. None of this was easy. My whole life had been spent building up a shield – an external persona of pure strength – and a part of me was mentally fighting these decisions all the way. There was a great feeling of shame and guilt, like I had failed on some level in needing help from someone else. Like I was no longer strong enough. Googling therapy sessions confused me even more; all the options that came up felt overwhelming. I put my phone down and walked away, then forced myself to go back.

'Alex, you need to commit to this,' I told myself fiercely.

I ended up booking a session with someone who was based close to me. I had no idea where to start but the description of what this therapist did seemed to match some of the issues I thought I needed to address: depression, anxiety, substance abuse, the list went on. At least he named things I could understand, rather than just using terms like 'CBT therapy' that I had never heard of and made me want to run in the opposite direction. If I'm being totally honest, people had mentioned to me before that perhaps I should try therapy. I'd always met them with a mindset of 'why do I need someone who doesn't even know me to tell me about myself?'. Plus, I had this horrible vision of being sat in a room with a stranger who was trying to get me to open up while replying solely to what I was saying with 'yes' or 'no'. It's very hard for me to open up unless I click with someone.

Unfortunately, that's exactly how I felt in my first therapy session. The therapist was perfectly pleasant but I knew straight away I wasn't comfortable and that he wouldn't really be able to help me. I know now it can take a couple of goes to find the right person. And I'm so glad I didn't give up. A few days passed after that first disappointing experience, and I was still thinking over what I should do next. Then it hit me: Kelly had gone to see a guy in London every Friday for therapy sessions, and she had spoken to me regularly about the organisation behind it. Sporting Chance had been set up by former Arsenal and England captain Tony Adams, to support current and former elite athletes with everything from addiction to general mental health problems. Maybe this was the answer. I reached out to Sporting Chance and in two days was put in contact with a therapist named Nick. Nick became my angel, sent to me when I needed help the most.

The media likes to say that trolls 'forced' me into

therapy. That's not true. The trolls were a catalyst for my breakdown, but I'd been struggling long before I was getting abusive messages on social media. While writing this book, I made a timeline of my life, which I've never done before. I couldn't believe what I was reading back when it was all written out in black and white. 'FUCK!' I said, laughing out loud to myself. 'No wonder I ended up in therapy.' From 2012 to 2018 I'd moved countries twice, seen the end of an eight-year relationship that started when I was nineteen, been in a near-fatal car crash, lost my starting spot in the England team after a decade, retired from football full stop, begun a new broadcasting career in a field traditionally pretty hostile to women – the list seemed to be endless. And that was on top of the scars left by my childhood.

I don't write this to try and gain sympathy for my trauma – because let's call it what it is – but to show that this stuff builds up. I didn't deal with those things head on; I couldn't. They went in my little box. But they were part of *life*. This kind of stuff happens and no matter how happy you are, how resilient your can-do attitude, sometimes you really cannot go it alone. So many fantastic things were happening in my life at the same time as everything I've just detailed, but not processing the hard bits made my whole world grey.

What did that look like in practice? When my nan died in 2017, I couldn't face going to her funeral. Along with Mum, Nan was the most important woman in my life. I'd spent every other day with her as a child. Her illness hit me like a ton of bricks, partly because she'd hidden how serious it was from us, right up to the moment she went to hospital. That was so like her; she was always looking after everyone else (writing this now, I'm starting to understand more about where I might have learned some of these lessons . . .).

The last day I had with Nan in hospital, I remember holding her hand. She was talking to me about the places I had visited in the world and then she paused and just said: 'I'm proud of you.' It was the sort of loving talk that we don't really do in my family, so immediately it made me emotional to hear her say those words out loud to me. Eventually I had to go as I had football the following day, and the next morning the call came: Nan was gone. I lay in bed crying for a bit but then had to get myself together – I had football.

Her funeral was a few days later but when it came down to it, I just couldn't face it. I couldn't process Nan being gone. Not the woman who had helped raise me, who'd spent so many hours cooking with me, braiding my hair, regaling with me stories about Jamaica, her life, her world. How could she not be here anymore? I told Mum and my brother I would meet them at the church but I never made it. Instead, I spent the whole day crying on my own. I didn't want to say goodbye. Eventually, I dragged myself to my car and drove to Nan's house in Wapping where the family was meeting for drinks and a celebration of her life. It felt so wrong to be in Nan's house without her there to greet me, and to this day I haven't set foot inside that house again because I simply can't do it. I miss her too much.

My dad was at the wake, of course, as Nan was his mum. It was the first time I'd seen him since he turned up at an England game of mine in 2014 after I'd had that near-fatal car crash. I remember him approaching me on the balcony, at the entrance to Nan's house, where I'd headed so people wouldn't see me cry. The balcony was where I would always knock on the door, waiting for Nan to open up and see my smile. Only once I'd said 'Hi Nan, it's me' would she hurry back into the house to fetch her keys and unlock the black iron gate that covered the doors and windows to deter any intruders. To distract from all the metal, Nan always had flowers placed along the balcony, to bring in some colour. When Dad approached me, I could tell he'd been drinking. Just like when I was younger, no matter how much he tried to disguise it with his eyes, his speech always gave him away, slurred and slow. For the first time, I wasn't hit with the need to impress him or worry about him. I was broken at the loss of Nan and had this brave, cocky feeling that I'd never experienced around him. I wasn't 'little Alex' at that moment. Dad said he'd made a lot of mistakes in his life but he still had a chance to make them right. To be honest, it all sounded great and I thought, 'OK, I may actually hear from him a bit more going forward.' But I never really did. In retrospect, maybe that opened up a few more wounds. Working with Nick later, I examined my relationship with Dad in great, uncomfortable detail. Nick took me back to the root of how I conducted my adult business, a direct result of never speaking about, or dealing with, how I felt about my childhood and growing up. I hadn't been given a space to discuss or process the impact of my childhood because it was always too raw for the people around me. We had to just keep going.

It was a lesson I'd internalised and applied no matter the situation. Take an incident that took place at the 2018 Russian World Cup. Strangely, I start this story with a smile – I'm lucky to have some really good people in my life, and two of them work at the BBC: Louise Sutton and Steve Rudge, who I mentioned earlier. These two have been there as mentors and friends from day one of my broadcasting career and I couldn't be more grateful. In 2018, they believed in me enough to push for me to head off to Russia as part of the official BBC punditry team. According to the various questions thrown at me on a press day in the lead-up to the tournament, I was going to be the first female pundit commentating at the World Cup. I didn't really think much about this at the time. I didn't want to be seen as a 'female pundit' – just a pundit full stop. Don't get me wrong, I was really proud of being part of the team, but that pride came from the fact I'd worked so hard on my degree, doing hours of placements, and now, in defiance of all the people who'd said there would be no place for me on TV because of my accent, here I was, off to a World Cup for the BBC.

I had initially been contracted to do three live games

and some hits and features, which felt like a huge role. But I ended up doing far more. My first game was alongside Mark Chapman, Phil Neville and Didier Drogba. Chappers is one of the best at what he does; before the match he told me that today was a 'big deal' so he was going to come to me first and ask about the French full backs. He knew exactly what he was doing! I was in my element chatting about the full backs and felt totally at ease. And coming off the show I saw why Chappers had made sure he'd played to my strengths – the reaction was huge. I'd become this face of change. It was an enormous pressure. I didn't sleep much that trip; I was so anxious to live up to the responsibility I felt, to be twice as good as what was expected of me. I did have one night off though. But it didn't go quite as planned. In fact, I thought I was going to die.

Before going to Russia, the entire BBC team had been given numerous safety briefings, including on the racism and gendered violence there. But having been there for over three weeks, the atmosphere felt magical. It was one of the best environments I've been in: fans from all over the world had converged on the city, giving Moscow a carnival feel. Most mornings I would go for a run, and then, before going on air, take a stroll across a bridge near my hotel, just for some me time. I'd completely forgotten about the dangers we'd all been warned about and subsequently let my guard down. It nearly cost me. That particular day was a packed one. I had a live game in the afternoon, drinks with a friend in the evening – and in

the morning? Well, I was meeting Vladimir Putin, fresh
into his fourth term as President of Russia. As part of
the FIFA Legends programme, Rio Ferdinand and I had
been invited to the Kremlin to discuss the World Cup. I
was the only woman in the room – which, behind the
scenes, I think had caused some anger because of the
politics involved in sitting with certain world leaders. But
I was there to discuss football. I even learned a sentence
in Russian, which I attempted and failed, but God loves
a trier!

The whole morning was utterly surreal. We snapped
pictures with Putin, but I was scared to even eat the tea
and cake in front of me in case I unwittingly broke some
unspoken diplomatic convention. Rio made me laugh on
the way out – he opened his hand to reveal he'd nicked
a teaspoon as a memento. But there was almost no time
to process my visit to the Kremlin – it was straight on to
the live game and, when that was done, into a BBC car
to meet my friend in a hotel across the city. After a few
drinks I had to leave as I had filming the next day. Normally the BBC are very strict about us taking pre-booked
cars from A to B for safety reasons, but I only had a
fifteen-minute journey back to the hotel and was feeling
comfortable enough in Moscow that I made what would
turn out to be a notably bad decision. I booked an Uber.

Climbing into the car, the backseat was full of junk –
the driver looked at me and in broken English told me
to 'come in the front'. I didn't even think about it. I just
hopped in. I heard the door lock and off we went. A few

minutes into the ride, my Uber driver pointed to his mobile, which was lodged in a phone holder in the middle of the car and explained that his English was not good, so he was using Google Translate.

'No problem,' I laughed. 'Broken English is fine.'

He was a stacked bald man, stocky, and wearing a grin on his face while making small talk. I was tapping out a message on WhatsApp when he looked at me and said – in English – 'Tell them they will never see you again.'

I stared at him, thinking he must have said or meant something else.

'Excuse me?' I said with a nervous giggle.

'You never see them again,' he repeated.

'I don't understand,' I stammered.

My Uber driver picked up his phone and spoke into it, waiting for me to see the words as they appeared via Google Translate.

'Tonight I am not taking you home,' the translated text read. 'You come with me.' My body went numb. He looked over and said, 'Yes.'

'I can't do that,' I replied, voice shaking. 'I need to go home.'

Through broken English and Google Translate he began telling me horrible, terrible things: how he takes girls like me, how they never make it home, what he would do to me. A million thoughts were racing through my head: how the heck had I been so stupid? Can I try to run at the next set of lights? But wait, no, the doors are locked. Fuck . . . FUCK! What am I going to do?

The driver hadn't taken my phone, and I messaged my agent Jake with my location and told him if I wasn't back in fifteen minutes to send a search party. Jake thought I was drunk and messing around, while I tried to explain that I was in an Uber and the driver was scaring me. I didn't want the driver to pick up on how panicked I was – I had a sense that would only feed his enjoyment of the power he currently held over me. Jake started ringing me, asking what was going on. I couldn't say it out loud; I felt like it would escalate the tension to a place I really wouldn't be able to come back from if I said I was being kidnapped. I just said I was on my way home and would be back soon. I don't think I've been in a worse situation to this day: Jake on the phone, laughing at me, telling me I'm drunk, while the Uber driver on my left continued to grin and tell me: 'No, you coming home with me.'

I hung up the call with Jake. The Uber driver spoke into his Google Translate again. The text swam into focus on the screen. This time it read: 'Girls like you I kill.' I could tell he wasn't messing about.

'Oh my god,' was my first thought, a wave of sadness crashing over me. 'I'm never going to see Mum again.'

I'm one of those people who, once they've visited a place, can get their bearings. We weren't driving in the direction of my hotel, but instead further and further out of town. Through my fear, I spotted the Kremlin in the distance. Suddenly a lightbulb flicked on: Putin! I had been with Putin that morning!

I turned back to the driver, now full of confidence.

'You can't kill me,' I said. 'I have to see Putin tomorrow.'

He started laughing.

'No one sees Putin,' he replied.

'I promise tomorrow I do, look, LOOK!' I was scrambling now, pulling up photos from the morning's visit to the Kremlin that had made newspaper headlines. His laughter died and I could see the cogs whirring as he tried to process what I was showing him.

I knew this was my escape and doubled down.

'See?' I said. 'You can't kill me. If I don't see Putin tomorrow, he will find you.' It was dialogue right out of a movie, and how I managed to remain outwardly calm in the situation I will never know – I have never felt terror like it. You don't know fear until your life is truly in danger. But it worked. Within seconds we were heading back to the city and towards my hotel. As we pulled up, I could see some BBC staff I recognised walking up the steps. 'Look, they're waiting for me,' I told him. The driver parked up abruptly, trying to touch my legs and pull me in for a kiss, but one of the staff members spotted me and began walking towards the car. I heard the door unlock and scrambled out – I was free. Then I briefly recounted what had happened to my colleague, said it was 'no big deal' and went to bed. Classic Alex. If I don't think about it, it hasn't affected me, right?

The next morning, after hearing what had gone on, Jake apologised for thinking I'd been messing around.

He told me the same evening I'd escaped, a male member of the team hadn't been so lucky – after climbing into an Uber he'd been robbed, beaten and dumped. Thankfully he'd survived but was now on a flight back home to England. I knew then what a near-miss I'd had, but rather than confront it I just threw myself into my busy broadcasting schedule and brushed aside the incident like it had never happened. After all, I'd got out unharmed – physically, that is. And I certainly didn't tell anyone else outside of the immediate team about it. I didn't want people to worry about me or think I couldn't handle myself – just like when I was young.

After the World Cup, there was no rest; I came back and immediately debuted as the first woman on Sky Sports' Super Sunday. I'd wanted to just rock up, but the press got hold of the fact I'd be appearing and ran stories beforehand, hyping up the occasion. I got a lot of love but also, for the first time, the online trolling was overwhelming. People say 'ignore it', which would be good advice if only it were that easy. I didn't want to speak to Mum, the closest person to me, about it – I've always tried to shield her from more worry or stress in her life. I also worried that if I talked to my bosses about the impact the death threats and racist, misogynistic abuse were having on me, they would try and protect me by taking me off screen. Work was the one thing keeping me going – and removing me from the spotlight was exactly what the trolls wanted. I didn't want to be seen as a woman who couldn't handle being in a man's world.

So I kept absorbing the abuse and trying to pretend it wasn't affecting me. But it was, obviously. I'm human. I couldn't understand the hate I'd sparked. I was just doing something I loved.

The worst trolling I've received had to be when I was announced as Sue Barker's replacement for *Question of Sport*. I woke up to the headline in the paper just like everyone else telling me that, out of nowhere, I had this new job. Gary Lineker tweeted his congratulations to me to his millions of followers, which seemed to make it official in everyone's mind and set off the trolls to a whole new level. He had the nicest intentions and had no idea how much trolling and abuse I was already receiving. Although most of the headlines in the newspapers were positive, this happened at the height of the Black Lives Matter movement and I would guess that 90 per cent of the trolling was about race and a Black person 'taking' a job from a white woman.

My head manager had to get security on the case to protect me and see what could be done to control the situation. It seemed like I was the racists' number one target in the UK, all because of one job I had no clue about. I was trying to brush it all off but the abuse was constant and gathered momentum as the days went on. My management and the BBC bosses were supportive, calling me to express concern and check what they could do to help. After a few days, I was too scared to leave my house to go to the shop in fear of being verbally abused. It had gotten too much. But as I spoke to

Charlotte Moore, the BBC's Chief Content Officer, I had this moment. I can be quite shy on phone calls but suddenly I felt this inner strength and said, 'Charlotte, I don't need time off. I don't want to hide. If I'm not on screen across my normal roles, they will have won, I need to keep doing what I am doing and carry on, I will be OK.' Charlotte has always shown great faith in me and my career, which I am so grateful for, and she heard the urgency in my voice.

It was only after starting therapy that I began to open up. And I'm still learning how to. This book is an exercise in being vulnerable. But after several months of therapy, I started feeling like I was ready to begin speaking about how I was feeling – just a little bit. Nick was teaching me how to talk, *really* talk. I had a session with him one Friday morning, before heading off to Manchester for the *Football Focus* show. The next day, before going on air, I told Louise that I was ready to talk.

She didn't say anything much beyond: 'OK, Al, I support you.' Lou knows me so well, she knew that was all that was needed. If she'd said anything more, I might have changed my mind.

That *Football Focus* show was the first time I'd ever opened up on TV about what I'd been going through. Several times I had to stop, to hold back the tears, but Jermaine Jenas and Dan Walker were brilliant and kept stepping in to support me. Like everyone else, they hadn't known the extent of what I was going through, but once they found out, they were right there, lifting me up.

Jermaine said something during that show that gave me a fresh perspective I hold on to today.

'It's so wrong you're going through all that,' he said. 'But you are opening doors and others are following you. You will be remembered for that and that's why you have to keep going.'

I know that the trolling will probably never go away, not as long as the internet exists. But the amount of work I've done on myself means I don't care anymore. I'm part of wider change and am so proud of that.

What I realised after sharing that experience, and the outpouring of support I received, was that I didn't have to suffer in silence. There were a lot of people waiting to help me – I just had to be ready and find a way to ask for it. On my way home, Lou texted me a heart emoji. Sometimes no words are needed. The truth is, I'm messed up. Just like anyone else. You might see me on TV and think I've got my shit together – I don't! I'm still trying to get to grips with the way I operate and the things that go on in my head, so I can communicate them to others. But slowly, it's working. I know how to reach out now. And people around me understand that they may have to ask if I'm OK more than once, because the first time I will just say yes, no matter the truth.

I also recognise the warning signs of when I'm struggling now: I draw away from everyone, don't answer texts, and flat out don't want in-person conversation. I hide. Therapy doesn't 'fix' you but it does teach you how to deal with yourself. I still fight going to therapy. As I write this, I've been on a pandemic-induced break from my sessions with Nick, and those signs of struggle are rearing their heads again – I need him back in my life. And I'm OK with that.

I'm finding other ways to heal too. Doing *Who Do You Think You Are?* felt like therapy. Visiting Jamaica brought me close to Nan and to those feelings about my loss that I hadn't been able to confront until then. I feel so privileged that my job allows me these opportunities. It was much, much more than a TV show to me: it was in honour of Nan and her beautiful, vibrant life. I'd never been able to visit Jamaica before that, but suddenly, I was ready. I opened another piece of me up to the world.

I'll close this chapter with something I read the other day. I know that therapy isn't for everyone; it's not one-size-fits-all and might not be suitable, depending on your particular needs. But this resonated with me.

Myth: Therapy is for people who can't help themselves.
Fact: Therapy is for people who want to help themselves.

12

Strength Is . . .
Learning To Let Guilt Go

According to the internet, some of the signs you might be coping with a guilt complex include anxiety, crying and insomnia. The page at the top of my search results says emotional guilt is a 'self-conscious emotion that involves negative evaluations of the self, feelings of distress, and feelings of failure'.

I've been looking for a way to describe the guilt I carry. It's not the sort of guilt where I've personally wronged people (not that I've never wronged anyone, but I deal with that differently). My guilt comes from a constant fear of letting people down, of not being able to do enough to help them or even 'fix' their problems. I also feel indebted; like if someone believes in me or does something for me, I owe them – which is why I find it very hard to say no. But through therapy and interrogating these feelings, I'm starting to understand them more – and how practising saying no is one of the steps to letting this guilt go.

My guilt can manifest in dreams. For example, the other day I dreamed that something was wrong with my dad. In the dream, he was sick. Waking up in a panic, I called my brother Ronnie, asking him to reach out to Dad – as they're still in direct contact – and check he was OK. However crazy I seemed at that moment, Ronnie did as I requested. He reported back that Dad sounded OK.

I was flooded with guilt that I wasn't in contact with Dad myself, that I wasn't able to check on him because I've cut him off. I've always felt guilty when it comes to the relationship with my dad. Yet even when we did have sporadic interactions, *I* was the one who would pick the phone up after months spent resolving not to do so unless he got in touch – because what if he was feeling sad about our relationship and just waiting for me to contact him? What if something happened to him? How could I ever live with not having given him a chance? But through therapy, I began to sit with these feelings rather than acting on them. The fact was, I had given Dad many chances. Whenever I'd talk to him, I would hear lame excuses about why he never called: 'because I know how busy you are' or 'I don't even know if you're in the country'. I had to stop letting my guilt continue our relationship on those terms. It was worse for my mental health in the long run.

Dad isn't the only family member I feel guilty about. You know when you hear footballers or musicians talk about buying their mum a house? I love that. But it makes me feel a deep guilt that I haven't made enough money yet to do the same for my mum and brother. Every day I feel guilty that I've managed to 'escape' the house and area we grew up in – not because I'm ashamed of it, but because it's filled with memories that are hard to live with. Of course I share the good stuff I have with them as much as possible: we go out for lovely dinners, I take Mum to the theatre regularly, and a few years ago I managed to sort out our first ever family holiday – Center Parcs. We had the best time, but on the last day I watched all our moods take a downturn as the imminent return to reality hit. I felt so sad and guilty that I haven't been able to fully take Mum and Ronnie along with me, away from that house.

They don't need or want charity but I want them to have access to some of the things I have. I love to travel, for instance; my 'special place' is a juice retreat buried deep in the rural hills of Portugal. I go there to recharge, to think about anything and everything other than work and my constant carousel of worries about what I need to do for other people. I took Mum once and it was a special week. But Ronnie – who could do with a break more than anyone! – can't do things like that. A lot of people from my ends don't have a passport; they cost money and there's an unconscious worry about filling in paperwork. We didn't need one growing up as we weren't going on fancy trips abroad or doing the family holiday thing. It was through football that having a passport became a necessity for me.

I know a lot of this guilt says more about me than anything my brother or Mum might actually be feeling. But that's another problem – I don't *know* how they're feeling most of the time. I talk to Mum every day, she's my rock. Yet, for survival reasons, the three of us have grown up not confronting the worst memories. So we don't talk. And we also don't express love in the traditional way. I feel love and know I *am* loved, very deeply, by both of them. We're a unit. But abuse changes the way you feel you're able to express that love. We don't say it out loud.

I've been on a journey of therapy and self-discovery to deal with a lot of the things that haunt me. And I'm aware that just because I'm ready to confront certain ghosts doesn't mean my mum and brother are. But I have a saviour fixation – I want to *save* them. I'm not sure how they'll feel about that. It'll probably make Mum sad to read this. I'm not sure how Ronnie will react. We have the type of sibling relationship where I know we'll be by each other's side for whatever is needed, but we don't ring each other all the time and speak about life. I feel especially guilty where Ronnie is concerned though, because I was the lucky one: I had football as my escape and release throughout my childhood. But I think my brother struggled more with where life would take him – he was a promising footballer too, but then he got injured and started making the wrong choices.

We always spent Boxing Day at our nan's for Jamaican Christmas. It was the only time we would see the other members of Dad's side of the family really. Everyone would always talk about how well I was doing with my football and playing for England – they spoke to me with such positivity. But when they talked to Ronnie, it was in a different tone, and more about what he needed to do in his life and how he should be focused, and the talk would go on and on. Looking across at my brother I would always think to myself, 'This is a time to be celebrating and happy, not giving a lecture.' I would be filled with such guilt for seeming like this goody-goody, when actually I was crying out for family to talk to me about *me* and ask about Alex the person not Alex the footballer sometimes. And, Ronnie, if you're reading this, I may as well tell you how proud I am of you, how it's you by Mum's side every day, how you've raised a beautiful daughter as a single parent in a stable and loving environment, the opposite of what you had. Skye is so lucky to have you as her dad. You're the one that keeps me and Mum going. I just want you to know that. You've always been the best big brother to me, protecting me and Mum and showing up when you sensed I needed you the most, even if I couldn't say it out loud. Like when I lost Ella.

Ella was my baby. I can't express how much she meant to me – it was love at first sight. I didn't have any intention of getting a dog, but in 2007, Kelly wanted to go look at Boxer puppies. When we reached the breeder's house, I sat down and this little puppy waltzed over, before climbing into my lap. My heart melted. I knew she had picked me. Four weeks later, she was coming home with us. As I held her in the car, Rihanna's 'Umbrella' was on the radio and the hook stuck – so I named my little pup 'Ella'. For eleven years she was my shadow, my everything. No matter what happened to me, Ella was there. But in 2018, after spending four weeks in Russia for the World Cup, I headed to Mum's to pick her up and instantly knew something was wrong with her.

'What have you done with my dog, Mum?' I joked. 'She doesn't seem right.'

'You cheeky fuck,' Mum replied, before adding a little more sadly, 'She's getting old, Alex. She's slowing down.'

But I knew it was more than just slowing down – I knew my baby.

The next morning, I took Ella to the vet, and after examining her they couldn't look me in the eye. The news was bad. She had cancer and was bleeding out. They needed to operate first thing tomorrow. I was in shock. It seemed that 2018 was the year everything came to a head for me. I was returning from Russia to confront the end of a two-year relationship, and now, WHAM. I was faced with losing my best friend. I lay crying by Ella all night, awaiting the morning and praying she wouldn't leave me. As I dropped her off, she gave me a look. I sobbed and sobbed, driving to Mum's to await further news.

Six hours later, I got the call that broke my heart. The vet couldn't stop the bleeding and Ella's cancer had spread. She could only have days left and would spend them in pain if they woke her up from the anaesthetic. They told me what was best but I still had to give the go-ahead. I said I needed five minutes and hung up. Mum wasn't in the house, but Ronnie was. I called the vet back and said, 'I know what you have to do.' They told me to come and say my goodbyes. I was trying to be so strong, especially as Ronnie was there, but the tears were still falling.

'Don't worry, Ron, I'm fine,' I said, preparing to leave.

'Do you want me to come with you?' he asked.

'No, no, I promise I'll be fine,' I replied, tearily.

I went to the toilet to hide and have a little cry, then headed to my car. Ronnie was sitting in the passenger seat.

'I'm coming with you,' he said.

We drove to the vet's in silence. When we got there, they took me to see Ella – who was already gone. Everything hit me so hard. I was thinking about losing Nan the year before and just fell apart looking at Ella's little form. Now my shadow was gone too. Ronnie stood next to me, saying nothing at all, with his hand on my shoulder. I'll never forget the support he offered me that day. He didn't need words to comfort me. Just being there with me was absolutely everything.

I love nothing more than seeing my brother happy and able to have fun in life. Like me, I know he's struggled with depression. We've never talked about that; I worry if I was to broach the subject, maybe I'd lose him completely. But that probably says more about where my fear and guilt comes from than him. Nick says I have to stop feeling like Mum and Ronnie can only live life through me. They have their own worlds. It's difficult to put that into practice though; guilt is a trip.

I am getting better at managing it. I just want to open up our relationship more and share my life with them, not out of guilt but so we have the memories together. Ronnie came along for those 2021 birthday celebrations I mentioned after I begged him to. He had an amazing night – the fact he didn't get home until 5am felt like my mission was accomplished. But it's still difficult to stop constantly fretting that I'm not doing enough, or abandoning my family in some way by not being able to buy them a whole new life. I don't even think they'd want that – they've never asked me for it. They just want me to be happy.

Letting this guilt go is a lesson I'm very much still in the middle of learning. I'm doing better when it comes to indebtedness in my work, not thinking I 'owe' someone just because they were smart enough to recognise I could make them some money. But when it comes to family, it's different. Maybe that's love though. Always wanting to do more.

13

Strength Is . . .
Showing Your Softness

Music has been in my bones for as long as I can remember. I inherited it from my dad, who loved his music. His and Mum's first date was at the famous jazz club in Soho, Ronnie Scott's, which became my older brother's namesake. Music saw Dad at his best; I'd go with him when he went to buy new vinyl, and then when we came back he'd blast it while I danced around. Growing up, I was exposed to a hugely eclectic mix: reggae, jazz, pop, rock, blues – I loved it all.

Music has always been an escape for me. I felt it so deeply – listening to the likes of Nina Simone and *getting it*, even while being too young to understand exactly what it was I got; I just recognised all that soul and pain and emotion. Apart from all the other reasons I was gutted when my dad left, he also took his music collection and my favourite Nina Simone album with him. I would spend hours singing along to that album, into a little toy microphone I'd been given one Christmas. Later we found out he'd given his huge collection away, as his new partner didn't like or want it in her household. I cried over that; those records were everything to me and my brother. Why wouldn't he give them to us? It felt like a punishment all over again, like he didn't want us to have anything.

I went on to build my own music collection though. We used to have a CD man in Stratford, east London, who would import all sorts from America. I'd save up my pocket money and go visit him every Saturday. He'd tell me what album I needed and I'd rush home to play it on loop for hours. I loved it; I was always so far ahead of the music scene because of my CD man in Stratford. Maybe that's why I've always been good at the music round in pub quizzes.

As I got older, I found joy in heading out to concerts, musical theatre – and clubs. Loud music and dancing? You can't get a more perfect combination. You'd never catch me travelling anywhere without a Bluetooth speaker either; I was the unofficial Arsenal and England DJ.

So when the first series of *Strictly Come Dancing* aired on the BBC, Mum and I were hooked. It became our thing. Every year we'd watch the journey the latest crop of celebrities went on. The show felt magical, with its mix of live music and expression through dance. When I moved back to England from America in 2012, *Strictly* became part of a routine for me and Mum. We'd tune in week after week and then have a debrief to discuss who did well, our favourites and so on. That Christmas I knew exactly what Mum's present was going to be: *Strictly* tour tickets. I was gutted when I discovered they'd already sold out. People say that if you put a wish out into the world, you can manifest it, and maybe that's what happened. In interviews, when asked what TV shows I would love to do, my answer was always *Strictly*. But I never really thought it would happen – I didn't think the *Strictly* casting team would ever have a clue who I was. They also tend to have a lot more sportsmen than women. Every year I still dreamed of stepping on to that ballroom floor though. In 2018 I remember turning down *Celebrity SAS: Who Dares Wins*, even though I was an avid viewer, because I was still hoping for that *Strictly* call-up. I told my manager at the time that I wanted to 'hold out for *Strictly*'.

And then . . . it happened. January 2019, I got a call from Sara, part of a new management team I'd just started working with.

'Alex,' she said, 'you've been asked to a meeting with the *Strictly* team.'

I couldn't believe it – literally. One of my most ingrained protective mechanisms is not to get excited about things until they are fully confirmed or agreed. I tamp down all my anticipation to avoid feeling hurt or disappointed if something doesn't work out. Two weeks later I was in the Ham Yard Hotel, meeting two of the *Strictly* booking team. Straight away I felt at ease. I told them I couldn't believe I was actually getting to sit down and talk about maybe doing the show, given how much I loved it. As we parted ways, they said they would be in touch, but they had more meetings to get through and the whole thing is a big operation, like putting a puzzle together. I left feeling excited, like a kid at Christmas. A few weeks later I got the news: they wanted me. My cheeks hurt from smiling so much. All I could think was, 'Mum is going to be so happy!' After delivering the good news, Richard, the head of my team, slipped back into management mode.

'We don't normally know about *Strictly* so early,' he told me. 'But they know you have contracts, so they wanted to make sure you didn't get booked into anything and miss the opportunity.

'Hear me out,' Richard continued. 'I'm not sure you need to do it this year. You've got a lot going on and it may be better to wait for next year.'

I looked up at him and smiled. 'I think this year is the one, Richard.'

He gazed at me and said, 'OK, that's it then. You're doing *Strictly*.'

On the train home, I tried to process my emotions. I felt calmer and lighter, like it really was the beginning of a new chapter. I'd just begun therapy and now here was a fresh, exciting opportunity, one I'd been waiting for. It just felt right.

Telling Mum was wonderful, although I had to whisper the whole time and simultaneously calm her down as it was top-secret information. She knew the drill from when I did *Bear Grylls*, but her excitement at me going on our favourite show was so much that I had to remind her not to shout it from the rooftops. There was one person I dreaded telling, however, and that in itself was a sign. When it came to breaking the news to my then-partner, I was worried. I knew it would bring headaches – they were very jealous and would be worried about the so-called 'Strictly curse'. In retrospect, I think their jealousy was exacerbated by what we both knew deep-down: that our relationship was not long for this world. When you have all these signs in a relationship – like getting amazing news and not being able to tell your partner for fear of a row – why fight them? In the event, we broke up before *Strictly* started. Perhaps the curse is real after all – just not in the way the tabloids report it. Maybe even the thought of a commitment as intense as *Strictly* exposes the existing fault lines in a relationship.

Fresh off that break-up, I threw myself into *Strictly*. The build-up is so special – you get given a code name to avoid any leaks to the press, which I found endlessly funny. Mine was 'SuperGirl'. I remember going to my first fitting and trying on all sorts of dresses. I was so shy at that first session. I think people assume that athletes are really confident about their bodies but for me it's always been the opposite. High street fashion is not exactly designed for women who trained the way I did; I have big quads and a bum, so jeans and trousers would always get stuck. I mentally battle to understand that my body has been built to be strong for what I need it to do, and that it's carried me through a career so I should be proud of it. But it's more difficult to hold on to that when you're sitting next to a model at London Fashion Week or are in fittings for clothes made for a certain size or shape. Most women I know, whatever their body type, struggle with insecurities. I know I'm a 'conventional' size but that doesn't stop the voice in my head making me feel like an outlier when jeans I'm presented with by a stylist don't go over my quads. I saw a great quote from Dina Asher-Smith on her muscle tone and fashion that resonated. She said: 'Sometimes I'll pull on jeans, obviously I'm an athlete and the jeans won't get over my thighs. I'd never be upset by that; I just take the jeans off and think: "Stupid jeans", before finding another pair.' It's a mindset I want to achieve!

After my *Strictly* fitting, I allowed myself to really get excited. Everything was still top-secret – I had no idea who would be joining me on the journey. But I still had a big summer of broadcasting work ahead of me before the autumn, with the Women's World Cup. This time I'd been bumped up to lead pundit alongside Gabby Logan who was lead presenter. It was a huge moment for women's football; Gabby and I were both acutely aware of the importance that the quality of the broadcasting matched that of the men's tournament the year before. I learned so much from her during that summer; it's always funny how much chaos can be going on around us, and the audience at home won't know a thing. I confided in her about *Strictly* as well, as she'd done her own stint on the show and I wanted her advice. I've always looked up to Gabby as a mentor – anyone who wants to be at the top of their game should follow her example. Her recollections of her time on *Strictly* got me more and more excited.

Between therapy and some incredible new career milestones – like hosting *The One Show* for the first time and handing out a BAFTA – I was feeling more sure-footed than I had the year before. I wasn't 'better' yet but I was more myself.

In August, the line-up for *Strictly* was announced. I was the first female football player to appear on the show. I knew, once again, that I wasn't just representing myself; this was a massive new audience for me as well. Just because I was already across BBC and Sky Sports broadcasting didn't mean people knew my name. Mainstream BBC programmes are a whole different kettle of fish. I also knew I didn't come with a ready-made 'fan base' so my time on the programme could be extremely short. I just needed to enjoy it for what it was, however long it might last.

Even though knowing about my *Strictly* place so early gave me time to get some 'secret' dance training in, I opted not to. I wanted the full *Strictly* experience, from scratch. And besides, I could dance already – couldn't I? I thought at the very least I had some rhythm about me. Well, let me tell you, rhythm on the club dance floor does not necessarily translate to the ballroom. It's a different language altogether. We had our first couple of days of basic training in September and underwent the process of being paired up, which is a bit like speed dating. The celebrities basically have to dance with all the pros for a couple of minutes; it's all filmed and watched. From there, bosses decide who to pair you up with. It's quite intimidating because you finally realise how good the pros really are.

Straight away I got chatting to Kevin Clifton and Neil Jones; because they were both into football, the conversation was easy. I left the second day of basic training hoping I would be paired with one of them. It wasn't until the first day of filming for the launch show that we found out who our partners would be. I think everyone watching at home assumes that contestants already know who they're going to be paired with and the surprised reactions are all a big act. But I kid you not: you seriously don't have a scooby-doo. I remember waiting nervously under the spotlights for Tess Daly to announce who I would be working with . . . Neil Jones! Neil came sliding over on his knees. I was thrilled that I'd been assigned someone I knew would be easy to get along with. And I knew it would be a special process for Neil as well because it was the first time he'd been partnered on the main show.

I invited him to my mum's 60th birthday party two days later. It was a big occasion – I'd spent all the money I'd earned from covering the World Cup that summer on it (not the six-figure sum you might be envisioning). I thought it would be useful for us to spend time together, so Neil could learn about my life away from that of the Alex he might have seen on TV.

So my *Strictly* journey began in earnest. It was the first time I'd returned to the mindset of an athlete. Not so much the need to win at any cost, but to work hard and push myself to be the best I *personally* could be. I knew it would be unfair on Neil if I didn't put the hours in. I'd meet him in the dance studio at 9am and often wouldn't get home until 9pm. Then I'd watch videos of our training to try and bake it into my brain for the next day. Going into *Strictly*, there was a feeling that I'd have an advantage because I was an athlete. Unfortunately the opposite was true! Athletes are trained to keep everything tight and tense. Dancing is completely different; you have to learn to be soft and elegant in every movement, from hand placement to always pointing your toes.

I couldn't actually point my toes. I have no cartilage, thanks to a condition called osteoarthritis, which degenerates that natural cushion – eventually you end up with bone rubbing on bone which, believe me, is very painful. From my ankles down, I've got a lot of damage and have carried it since my footballing days, but I never let it stop me doing what I want to in life. Neil knew the seriousness of my injuries but I didn't want to make a thing of it while on the show in case people thought I was getting special treatment. I did all the week's dance training in trainers and would only switch to heels on Friday's dress rehearsal, which would cause a lot of pain.

Every time head judge Shirley Ballas would instruct me to point my toes in judging feedback, I would just stand there and smile while Neil squeezed my hand as if to say, 'Don't worry, we'll work around it.' I loved training every day with Neil and learning all the new moves. I was physically shattered though, and not just from dancing. Sundays were our only days off from the *Strictly* rehearsal schedule but I'd just taken over from Ben Shephard, presenting Sky's *Goals on Sunday*. I would get home from the *Strictly* live show on Saturday at about 2am and watch all the football I'd missed, waking up at 5am on Sunday morning to head to the Sky Sports studios for 6am. It's not a schedule I'd recommend. I'm not actually sure how I managed it, to be honest. You make it work at the time.

Plus, *Strictly* is an emotional rollercoaster. Come Saturday night, all the hours and hours of work you put in seem to melt away when you're standing in front of the judges. Of course they give positive feedback but all I could hear were the negative comments. By the third week it was starting to chip away at my already low self-confidence. That night, Stacey Dooley, the previous year's winner, was sitting in the live studio audience and after the show had finished, she called me over. Clearly she could see I was being down on myself because she gave me a Dooley-special firecracker pep talk.

'BABE, keep fucking going, OK?' she told me firmly. 'It's not about the judges, it's about everyone picking up the phone and voting for you, you dance for them.

'Look at me, I didn't get over twenty-three in the first three weeks and I went on to win the bloody thing. Keep your chin up. You're bloody amazing. OK?'

Stacey likely didn't know the effect her words had, but back in the changing room I had a little cry. I've always needed positive reinforcement to keep going and that message from Stacey was a wake-up call. The following week we'd been assigned the Charleston, which is such a fun dance. I realised it was also an opportunity to be confident in just being me. In previous weeks, I'd been trying to be 'Sassy Scott' and 'Sexy Scott' – we'd come up with different characters every week to try and help me through a dance. But I was trying to play roles I didn't feel totally comfortable in, and that was leaking through. From week five onwards, it was like I flipped a switch inside me: to ignore the noise, stop comparing myself to fellow contestants and be secure in the knowledge that what I could bring was equally as good and unique.

That Saturday I even plucked up the courage to say I didn't feel comfortable with my hairstyle. I told Neil my hair would be better in a bun, and that I could do it myself – so I did. When we hit the dance floor that night, it wasn't Alex trying to be anyone but Alex. That evening, Motsi Mabuse told me, 'Welcome to *Strictly*, welcome to the competition.' It felt good for one of the judges to see something in me. Funny though, because I never viewed it as a competition, at least not against others. The only person I was competing with was myself, as clichéd as that might sound. You didn't have time to think about the other contestants anyway; Friday was the first time you'd be reminded that they existed. Watching the likes of Karim Zeroual and Kelvin Fletcher, I thought: 'There's no way I could compete with them anyway.' So I resolved to concentrate on myself and just love doing my dance; then if any week ended up being my last, so be it.

I wasn't particularly looking forward to Halloween week. Neil and I had been assigned 'Ghostbusters' as our track and we'd had external choreographers come and prepare a 'street commercial' routine to accompany it. I was really keen to try the street commercial style but neither of us was particularly jazzed by the song choice. Nevertheless, we got on with it. It was one of the hardest dances of the series for me. It looked so simple to the audience at home but it was one of those where both you and your partner had to get every single step right. Neil and I put in our longest hours to date to nail it, and finally it felt like we had. If I'm keeping it real, it wasn't a dance I wholeheartedly loved, unlike the Charleston or the Paso Doble. But I felt so lucky the public had liked us enough to keep us in to that point, and besides, I'd learned how to moonwalk. Focusing on the positives had me smiling.

The Saturday of the live show dawned and we headed down for one final dress rehearsal, proton packs in hand. A few minutes into popping some moves though, I saw Neil jumping around. I knew instantly he'd pulled a muscle – I'd seen it so many times in my football career.

Immediately, people came running to assist him and poor Neil limped off to the physio's office. I had no idea what was going to happen. Stef, the *Strictly* talent booker, eventually found me and delivered the news: 'Babe, Neil is injured and can't dance.'

She told me the team had come up with a couple of options and the one they thought was best was carrying on with my performance – but with Kevin Clifton. I also had a get-out. 'You have every right to say no and not dance this week, then you will be automatically through to next week when we can see if Neil is better,' said Stef.

My first thought – classic Alex! – was that I didn't want to put anyone out or be seen as a diva by refusing to dance (looking back now, the sensible thing would have definitely been to take that option). So I replied, 'Yeah, no worries, I will just dance with Kev.' Ha! What a fool! Firstly, the point of *Strictly* is to build a strong relationship with your partner, so it's completely alien to suddenly start dancing with someone else in that way – a whole different language. Secondly, the routine was particularly hard, remember? If it had been a ballroom or Latin dance, Kevin would have been able to learn it in the forty minutes we had before going live, no sweat. But it was a nightmare routine, and so complicated. Picture me, taking Kevin through the moves, Neil sitting to the side trying to talk him through it. Kevin's a professional, a top-tier one, so he was picking it up, but suddenly time ran out. It was show time. I think you can have two mindsets: let yourself lean into the 'poor me' attitude and give up, or make the best of a bad situation. I mentally repeated my mantra: 'If this is my last dance on *Strictly*, I am going to go out loving every minute.'

I was still trying to teach Kevin the last few steps on the balcony as other couples took their turn on the floor. Then we were up. 'Enjoy, Kev,' I said with a grin, as the music started. We did the best we could; midway through the dance, I saw Kev blank on the next steps so I instinctively slipped into 'captain mode' and began shouting instructions across the dance floor. We were a team! I couldn't just leave him. The whole dance was . . . not the best, but when we got to the end, the music stopped and everyone was on their feet giving us a standing ovation. The audience had been told that Neil had been injured two hours before the show and they knew the dance was a mess. But what had been seen, and appreciated, was the attitude of carrying on and getting through. I got my highest score that week and it wasn't my last dance – the journey continued.

That word is associated strongly with *Strictly*: your 'journey'. It's often mentioned on the little montages they make for leavers and finalists. But it's not misused. In some ways, I felt I was lucky – not many people get to dance with two male pros in one season. With Neil still injured the following week, I remained paired with Kevin – and it was ballroom. I had it in my head, from previous weeks, that I was crap at ballroom. But Kevin got me to see beyond my doubts; he made me focus on the things I loved in the music because he wanted me to dance with freedom. When you see Kevin dance, you watch him get totally lost in the music. Between him and Neil I had two great teachers and even found myself loving the ballroom routines. What I felt in myself, and what I think people at home picked up on, was someone who started the show with very little proficiency and not much more confidence, but who was enjoying the process so much and growing as a person and a dancer. It was the first time I got to show the world more of me and my personality, beyond Alex the footballer or Alex the pundit. The *Strictly* viewers saw me laugh, they saw me cry; they saw someone living what felt like a fairy tale. And I did not want it to end.

Against what I thought were all the odds, we made it to Blackpool. For the *Strictly* uninitiated, once you get to a certain stage of the show, the remaining contestants go to Blackpool, to dance in the Blackpool Tower Ballroom. It's an iconic location for ballroom dancing and also huge. You go from dancing in a small, intimate studio at Elstree to dancing in this arena-sized space – it's electric. Neil had recovered from his injury and we were ready to go. A week before Blackpool he'd come to me and said that the team had suggested a song if we made it through, but he'd said no, yet wanted to check with me before the decision was final.

'What song is it?' I asked. He pressed play. Beyoncé's 'Run the World (Girls)' blared out of the speakers. I was gobsmacked. In my very first *Strictly* interview, the one artist I said I'd love to dance to was Queen B.

'Neil, I want to dance to this song,' I told him. 'I *have* to dance to this song.'

The great thing about being partnered with Neil was that he knew how much I loved music and he gave me the chance to weigh in on decisions when it came to our dance soundtrack. I'd picked and edited the music for our jive the week before. And I knew exactly which part of 'Run the World' we should be dancing to. I already had a vision in my head. At Blackpool, contestants always get more backing dancers and, throughout *Strictly* history, it usually ended up that a woman was surrounded by men. I wanted this dance to be about female empowerment and women taking control. Everyone who takes part in *Strictly* has a 'moment'; I told Neil this dance would be that moment for us. He 100 per cent bought into my vision and did everything to bring it to life. Because of his belief, it really did become my '*Strictly* moment' and one that I'll never forget. When all the women stalked out on to the floor, you could feel the energy in the room and knew the dance was going to be special. And when we incorporated Beyoncé's iconic shoulder shrug into the Paso Doble, the cheers erupted. To this day people still tell me how much they loved that dance. It had that full-on feminist feel, something I don't think had been done that unambiguously on *Strictly* before. Plus, I got my dream moment: I only went and danced to BEYONCÉ on *Strictly Come Dancing*. Come on now!

Blackpool also proved another milestone moment for me, in a much quieter way: it was the last time I spoke to my dad. He'd made some promises when I'd seen him two years earlier at Nan's funeral, promises that had never materialised. On the train to Blackpool, I was sitting next to Michelle Visage when I got a text. Out of the blue, Dad had messaged me, asking if he could get *Strictly* tickets . . . for two of his friends.

I was nearly a year into therapy at this point. For the first time, I actually expressed my feelings. I won't detail them here in full but I think you can guess what my emotional reaction was to being mined for tickets for people I didn't know, after two years of what felt like radio silence. I think it took Dad by surprise; he replied that the tickets were actually for him but that he didn't know how to ask me, which made me feel incredibly guilty – a feeling I'm trying to work past. But I quietly let it go. I didn't want to hold on to the anger and hurt. And I stopped reaching out – I haven't spoken to him since that exchange. Of course I want my dad in my life, but not at the expense of me.

Neil and I made it to week eleven of *Strictly*. Our last dance, a samba, was soundtracked by 'Joyful, Joyful' from *Sister Act 2*. It pretty much summed up my whole *Strictly* experience. The show brought a joy back into my life that I had lacked for a long time. During *Strictly* I learned that it's OK to show your vulnerabilities, to try something new and hard, and that it would pay off. It was also a reminder to be true to myself, to celebrate and roll with that. I was lowering my armour further and letting people around me see the softness at my core. I had achieved even more than I'd thought possible (I brought gospel to the *Strictly* floor!) and represented women's football on a massive new stage. Saying goodbye to *Strictly*, I really did feel for a brief moment like girls ran the world.

14

Strength Is . . .
My Mum

Dear Mum,

Here we are. Almost at the end of my book and this chapter is a letter to you.

Barely have I even started to write this and I'm already crying. Why? I think that, when I really allow myself to think about your life, I know you are struck with sadness, guilt and shame. No matter what goes on around you, it's like, deep down, you do not feel you can accept the happiness in your life. Like you're not worthy of it.

But you are, Mum. More than anyone else I know. I've been working on my own guilt a lot. I'll be honest, though, it still breaks my heart when I take you out for the lovely things you deserve, our 'fancy' meals, our theatre trips, those holidays. And even though we have a great time, I know that just below the surface, you don't feel like you should be sitting in that seat, surrounded by all those people. As if having nice things is not for someone like you because you're rooted in pain and suffering. I want to save you from it all. I know that's not possible. But I do.

What you can't see and accept is that you are a truly remarkable woman, Mum. You have an amazing ability to love and show kindness to everyone around you, except yourself. I don't want you feeling guilty about that either. I know you will see my sadness as a further source of shame. But I have to tell you this.

You are special. Everyone knows it.

It's ironic that I started this book talking about Dad and ended it with this letter to you. I said I don't hold on to anger, but maybe I lied because right now, writing these words, I feel so much fury inside me towards him. It's like he stripped you of certain things and you've never quite been able to get them back. The confidence in yourself you once had, the independence, the passion for life, the ability to let yourself be loved . . . These qualities might still be inside of you, but they are hidden, no longer easily accessible. I feel like I fail all the time, every day, Mum, because I haven't been able to help you get these things back. I know that's on me, those are my worries. But you are my centre of gravity.

Every interview I've ever done where I'm asked about my role model, it always comes back to you. You're my hero, Mum. You always will be. You saved me and allowed me to be the person I am today.

I would trade everything – all the trophies, the accolades, the career I have now – for you to be able to see this, experience some self-love and start to heal. Even a little.

Sometimes I get angry. I get these terrible thoughts,

like I want to shake you and say, 'You've still got so much life left! Please! Live!' and then I feel unbelievably selfish that I've even let that idea enter my head. I don't even really know how to talk to my therapist about this. I definitely don't know how to talk to you. I get frustrated with myself and end up saying nothing. A lot of the time we sit in silence together because we can't communicate, not with so much left unsaid. It's easier for us to stay in our heads.

Dad took away your ability to communicate your emotions. It hurts me to think an individual can be that powerful, can do that to someone. When I think about it, he did that to me too. But I was younger and, thanks to you, and my escape via football, I had the chance to start healing. You didn't.

You said something to me the other day that stuck with me. A rare insight into the level of pain you carry. You said you wished that you were able to enjoy the feeling of having young kids, to be able to love and hug your kids whenever you wanted. The fact he wouldn't even let you do that, that we weren't allowed to receive that love from you as children . . . I'm sorry, Mum, I really am.

But at the same time, we developed a bond so strong, we could communicate without words. Your children were your lifeline, Mum, and you were ours. You told me that story of being in the car with Dad. You were driving, with Ronnie and me, as babies, strapped in the back. All you could think of was running the car into a brick wall and ending the life you felt so trapped in. The thing that snapped you out of that moment was hearing my little voice from the backseat, trying to shout 'Ma!'. You shook off your plans to leave this world because you had us to live for.

You, me, Ronnie . . . we've all learned to live life not showing any vulnerabilities. I can't carry on like that anymore. I want us to break the cycle. Showing vulnerability is not an invitation for others to exploit it, it's being honest. For me to be honest, I needed to write this book and set myself free from all this pain, all this trauma. I needed to stop pushing it all away like it never happened.

I also want to apologise, Mum. I've been on this therapy journey, trying to find and understand myself more. In doing so, I tried to make you open up, tried to get you to where I was. I wanted to hear answers sooner than you were ready to give them. Looking back, that was selfish of me. I was trying to peel a plaster off a wound that was still raw and it took you back to that place. I'm sorry for that.

I need to tell you something else, Mum. One of the most heartbreaking things of all is that you think you're a coward. Not a day goes by when I don't hear your voice in my head or picture you telling me that you're a coward. You hold on to this untruth because you think it's your fault you didn't leave Dad earlier. As if it was that easy. Yet you still think if people find out what happened, that's how they'll look at you. Like you weren't brave enough.

I hope you're still reading, Mum. I looked up the word coward. It means 'a person who is completely lacking the courage to do, or endure, dangerous or unpleasant things'.

How could you ever be a coward? Can't you see you're anything but? You endured every dangerous and unpleasant thing possible for the love of your kids, Ronnie and me. We know this, Mum, we saw it. And even after what Dad did to you, you've always tried to protect him too. Today you can stop. He can't, and won't, hurt you anymore, Mum. Ronnie and I will always be there for you. You don't have to live a life in fear.

My friends have never really understood why I don't like birthdays or Christmas much. I've even got to the stage where I remove myself from them altogether (who's the coward now? I'm the one running, Mum). But those occasions are painful for you, and therefore me. Losing Nan just made them more so.

I could always sense your sadness on these occasions. You felt like you'd failed us because we hadn't got the latest toys or newest trainers, so you'd get yourself into more debt to make sure the cupboards were fuller than normal, with sweets and extra chocolate. Before we even opened a present, you'd apologise to us, saying you were sorry because it may not be what we were hoping for.

I hated this process of present opening and watching you trying to hide your sadness. I even got into the habit of going on a run beforehand, to brace myself mentally for what was about to happen. But when the presents were done, we'd do the bit I loved – and still do. We'd sit down together for dinner. We know how much you love your roasts! And you know how much joy Ronnie and I get from eating your home-cooked food. Who needs presents when you have that? That's all we need, Mum, to see you smile. It's all I've ever wanted. Let me be the one to shower you with gifts and great times, to treat you like the queen you are. In return, I just want to see you happy.

I don't know if you're even reading this, or if I'm getting across everything I want to say. But can you really put three decades' worth of emotion into one letter? I guess it boils down to this: Mum, please stop suffering for things in the past. I need you to want, and to try, to start living again. Please, for me. All I want is to see you smile more, for you to get on the phone to me and tell me you've had a good day, or a good time. I want you to find some light in the darkness. I'll be that light if you need me to.

Your soul is the purest one I've ever encountered. I want it to shine so you can feel the warmth we all do from being around you, even a little bit.

We've got a new chapter to face together - and I mean *together*, Mum, you're not alone. MS, the doctor said. Well. Life really likes to throw things at us, doesn't it? I know it can drive you a bit crazy because I'm really into mindsets and trying to find the positives in life. But I learned that strength from you, even if it's manifested differently. You shielded us and gave me the capacity to do that. This

MS is just another one of those things that we will deal with together.

The truth is, Mum, I need you. No matter how independent and fierce I may seem, I have always needed you and always will. So don't go and give up on me now, OK? I need you to fight this one last battle from within and show that courage you've always had.

This whole time, you've been strong for Ronnie and me. Let us be strong for you. Let us show you how not to be strong, Mum.

I hope this book helps set you free. I LOVE YOU, MUM. Forever. To the moon and back again.

Alex x

15

Strength Is . . . Having The Courage To Follow Your Dream

Just as this book was going to print, the Lionesses won the UEFA Women's Euro for the first time, changing the face of the women's game in this country. To understand the significance of that win, you really have to go back to 1999.

1999 was an iconic year in women's football. The USA won the World Cup, beating China in front of a record-breaking crowd of 90,000 people and with an estimated 90 million Americans watching on TV. In the US, the women's team became household names and their victory even led to Mia Hamm creating the first boots for women (I had a pair!). The 99ers – as that famous US team are known – didn't rest on their laurels, though. They knew they had to use their momentum to fight for change and to push the women's game on to another level. They established the first women's soccer league, called WUSA (after the Women's United Soccer Association), and negotiated the first collective bargaining agreement which made soccer a viable career in the US for both Americans and players like me. Every young girl in the US wanted to be just like the heroes they saw lift the trophy in that World Cup Final, and the 99ers played a vital part in changing the face of women's football around the world.

I saw the American crowds on TV but it felt like another world to the council estate I lived in and the grounds I was playing on. In 2007, England qualified for our first World Cup in twelve years under Hope Powell, and we made the quarter-final. It was a major success but we had to do even better. We knew that every time we made a quarter-final or final, like in 2009, it allowed Hope to bang on doors (many were slammed in her face) for more investment for women's football. We might get a small news item or a headline. Bit by bit, we knew it all made a difference.

My generation of Lionesses reached the World Cup for the third time in 2015. We got knocked out at the semi-final by Japan, but we knew that getting those bronze medals around our necks allowed us to push for more funding for the game and for the WSL. Hope always said that it was about turning that silver medal in 2009 into a gold. We wouldn't stop until we got there, but we knew we couldn't do it without much more support. WSL teams needed more investment and we needed more backing and support from men's clubs, otherwise we would be stuck as just that semi-final team every time. If our domestic league wasn't the best in Europe, or the world, we would always stay at this stage, so close and yet so far.

When we won the bid to host the 2022 Euros, the FA asked me if I could be part of the board to represent the players' perspective. I was there for the planning, the disappointments, the small wins and the dreams and, ultimately, the vision that we could make this the best European Championship the women's game had ever seen, even with all of the obstacles – like a pandemic – that were thrown in the way. Covid had hit the game bad. Beth Mead had to go on Twitter and ask for an exercise bike just so she could train and stay fit.

As we got closer, we started thinking, 'What if . . . ?' BBC and Sky Sports were now showing WSL games every weekend so audiences were beginning to recognise players and follow their journeys. Tickets went on sale and the Lionesses' games all sold out. Then the final at Wembley sold out too, without anyone knowing who would be playing. Even before the tournament started, Lionesses were plastered everywhere: on bus stops, crisp packets and billboards. You couldn't go anywhere without knowing that the Euros were about to start. I thought, 'This is how it should be.' 'Just imagine, just imagine,' we would say. 'The Lionesses at Wembley in a final . . .' I would shake my head when the thought flashed through my head. But, ever Alex, I never allow my mind to get carried away into the future; I have to deal with the now. And the now was shouting about women's football from the hilltops.

The opening night at Old Trafford was special. I was honoured not only to be part of the BBC coverage but to be part of the crowd cheering on the team to their first win. As the match finished, Gabby Logan turned to me with a smile on her face and asked me if I was OK. I shook my head with disbelief and said, 'This is it, Gabby. This is it.' The crowd, the atmosphere, Beth Mead giving the Lionesses their first win of the tournament ... It was all underway, and it felt like we were heading into a magical summer of women's football.

Every England game thereafter seemed to fall into place. No one would have ever guessed that England would beat a strong Norway team 8-0. The super subs made their own stories and headlines as we played Northern Ireland. It looked like it might be all over as Spain had us against the ropes but in Sarina Wiegman we trust – and in Ella Toone and Georgia Stanway. The Lionesses found it in themselves to come back. Then, somewhat unbelievably, England breezed into the final beating the second-ranked team in the world, Sweden, including one of the goals of the tournament, a cheeky back heel from Alessia Russo that even prompted my longtime hero Abby Wambach to tweet wishing she had scored a goal like that in her career.

We witnessed a true team performance with every single player contributing to the greater good. Good teams become great teams when members trust each other enough to surrender the me for the we, and that is what we all witnessed in the Lionesses. Ian Wright and I could not hide our emotions with goal celebrations and impassioned calls for change in the game. Crowd records were being smashed and everyone on the streets was talking about the women's game. As the sun shone up and down the country, it finally felt like after almost sixty years, football could finally come home.

It felt written in the stars that it was meant to be England vs Germany at Wembley. And it was in front of a record crowd for any Euros final: 87,192 people, not to mention the 17 million watching at home. Going into extra time was agonising. Surely the Germans were not going to cause the nation heartache and stop these amazing Lionesses achieving their dream, were they? It was now or never for the Lionesses. Having fought her way back into the team after suffering a serious knee injury, Chloe Kelly was quick to react from a corner and poke the ball home into the back of the net, giving the England team a historic win in a historic tournament.

History has a way of repeating itself. Just as Brandi Chastain, the famous 99er, had done in the 1999 win, Kelly's celebration was to whip her top off. Kelly was still a baby when that iconic match took place but, as I stood in the studio witnessing the scene in front of me, crying, I remembered that moment. I knew that just like the US's 1999 win, this would allow the England team to change women's football in this country. It felt like a win not only for the current Lionesses but for every woman who'd worn the England shirt before, and every single person who has been fighting behind the scenes for decades. Fighting to push the women's game forward and to change perceptions has been my life's work and it has been exhausting at times, but at the final whistle, I felt the team had finally changed the game forever. No going back. My friend Leah Williamson, the team captain, summed it up perfectly when she said, 'This is not just the end of a tournament but the start of the journey.'

The day after the win was one of those 'pinch me' moments that I never thought I would witness as people packed into Trafalgar Square for the victory parade. I was flattered that the FA and BBC asked if I would host live on BBC One. I was overwhelmed and overjoyed. In between my TV duties, I kept running to the corner to the team and crowds as I was just so proud to watch them have that moment. The next day, as I recovered from the worst (but best!) hangover of my life, I lay on my sofa and saw the letter the Lionesses had addressed to the government demanding change. It demanded that every young girl have the opportunity to play football in schools. A proud smile spread across my face. What the Lionesses have done is change perceptions, not just in football but in society. This was not just a win for an England team but a win for women's sport around the world.

Gabby Logan signed off the game saying, 'You think it's all over; it's only just begun.' Never a truer word said. It's only just begun.

I said live on air as I took in the celebrations, 'The train has well and truly left the station and it's gathering speed.'

The next chapter of football starts now . . .

Conclusion

I recently went on a trip with UNICEF to Namibia for a Soccer Aid appeal film, another of those eye-opening travel opportunities I've mentioned throughout this book. While there, I visited hospitals and social projects and met a lot of young women, all of whom needed support in different ways. On my last day there, I met a sixteen-year-old named Venessa, mother to three children, all under the age of four. I won't mince words; her life was one of hardship. Venessa had been raped; after the assault, she was forced to leave school and care for her children. She had no income; Soccer Aid donations were enabling local healthcare personnel to make sure mothers like Venessa were able to keep feeding their babies. The conditions Venessa lived in were bleak but there was still hope, and the film we were making was designed to show that.

As filming wrapped on the last day, I looked over the scrubby landscape and saw Venessa in her smart black dress, outside her house, one of her babies on her hip. A wave of feeling crashed over me; I knew I had to walk back and speak with her off camera. As I approached, she looked up and smiled. I thanked her for her time and reinforced how powerful she had been in articulating her story. Her words, I said, would hit home with millions of people around the world, no matter their circumstances.

In reply, Venessa said something totally unexpected.

'Alex, can you wait here one moment, please?' she asked, softly. 'I have something I want to give you.'

Taken aback, I said, 'Of course.' I watched her turn and head into the house, pausing to pick up what looked like a folded piece of paper. Then she was on her way back to me, holding out the paper.

'I wrote these words over a year and a half ago,' Venessa said. 'I knew from the moment I met you, I was meant to give this to you. Read it when you are ready, but it's for you.'

Surprised didn't even cover it. I didn't know at all what to say, but I managed a 'thanks' and to express that I looked forward to reading whatever she'd written. We said our goodbyes and I rejoined the crew, hopping on to the minivan that would take us to the airport. My head was already back in England; I felt burnt out once more and ready to escape life and people. Settling into my seat, I unfolded Venessa's letter.

It read:

Are you full of energy? Do you think you can conquer the world? You know what? You can. But it's not easy, you have to prepare yourself whole inside and out. Be ready for whatever comes, because the real journey starts now.

Associate yourself with those that challenge you. Don't try to be the best, try to be the best version of yourself. Remember don't be Miss/Mr Know It All because what one does not know, someone else will know. When we are young we often have the energy but do not know how to use it and as we get older we are less hungry and ambitious for certain things.

When looking from a different perspective we tend to see ourselves less and this kind of negativity is always affecting our life really badly. When aiming for something, we should cut out anything that would hinder us from being successful. Even if it means cutting out people who are close to us, especially if they are negative. In this life we have to make huge sacrifices even if it's difficult. It is never easy, it will never be easy but it has a reward in the end.

To find what you seek in the road of life, the best proverb of all is that which says: 'leave no stone unturned'. Don't worry about making mistakes. No matter how perfect it may get, you will always make mistakes because they are part of life. Besides, a life making mistakes is not only honourable but more useful than a life spent doing nothing.

I slowly refolded up the letter and tucked it carefully away into my pocket. My fatigue lifted for a moment; my heart felt warm and huge in my chest. In the most Walt

Disney way possible, I knew that those words at that exact moment in time were exactly what I needed to hear. I felt like the universe had delivered me that letter from Venessa for a reason, to share her wisdom with you all, here. If Venessa can manage to find the light – and pass that light forward – then we all can.

The writer Joseph Campbell said the following: As you go down the path of transformation, of trying to become your ideal self, you are going to meet a part of yourself that you don't want to be; you will see all your flaws, all the things that caused you pain.

This book has been the first time I have reflected on a lot of things in my life and hopefully every chapter shows how having strength and being strong can be so different in so many ways: it can be hard, it can be soft, you can find it in loss, or in others – it comes in so many forms. For me, learning how not to be strong is a celebration and an achievement of finally being able to see me.

Are you full of energy? Do you think you can conquer the world? You know what? You can!
But it's not easy, you have to prepare yourself whole, inside and out. Be ready for whatever comes, because the real journey starts now.
Associate yourself with those that challenge you. Don't try to be the best, try to be the best version of yourself. Remember don't be 'miss/mr know it all' because what one does not know, someone else will know. When we are young we often have the energy but do not know how to use it and as we get older we are less hungry and ambitious for certain things.

When looking from at a different perspective we tend to see ourselves less and this kind of negativity is always effecting our lifes really badly. When aiming for something we should cut out anything that would doing hinder us from succeeful. Even if it means cutting out people who are close to us, especially if they are negative. In this life we have to make huge sacrifices even if it's difficult, it this life never easy it will never be easy but it has a reward in the end. To find what you seek in the road of life, best proverb of all is that which says, 'Leave no stone unturned'.
Don't worry about making mistakes, no matter how perfect u may get you will always make mistakes because

they are part of life. Besides a life making mistakes is not any honrauble but more useful than a life spent doing nothing.

Acknowledgements

Wow, and just like that I've come to the end. Or rather, the end of this chapter of my life. Hopefully you understand me a little better than you did at the start of this book.

I want to start by thanking YOU. You, who decided to pick up this book and were invested in me enough as a person to want to know more. All of you that have cheered for me, shown support, stopped me in the street or shouted nice things from afar. It really means so much.

Here's a story about that. I remember during lockdown, I would jump on my bike and make the trip from north-west to east London to visit my mum in her 'bubble'. The sun would be shining, while London was quieter than I'd ever seen it, eerily so. I'd ride along the Embankment, music in my ears, staring out at the beautiful city landscape and feeling so lucky. In all my years as a London girl, I'd never experienced it in this way.

My route took me through Wapping, and memories of Nan would come flooding back as I cycled along. I'd pass Chrisp Street Market in Poplar, where I spent many a Saturday afternoon visiting the pie and mash shops, or eating a Wimpy burger if Mum had the extra money, or went shopping for bargains at the market stalls. Once I reached Mum's I would have a cup of tea in the garden, make sure she was fine, then cycle all the way back home. One day, on that return journey, two older Black women were sitting on a bench in a part of Wapping. They saw me on my bike and were waving like mad. I thought they must be waving at someone behind me – I always assume no one recognises me – but there wasn't anyone there, so I stopped my bike and paused the music.

'Alex, Alex!' one of the women shouted over. 'Alex, my dear, we love you on *The One Show*. You keep going, you hear, you stay strong.' Even as I write this, I can't help but smile so widely at the memory. I think of Nan and feel like I'm making her proud, like she is looking down on me. In the moment, however, I was taken aback. At first, all I did was wave and shout 'Thank you', then continue on my way home. But once I began pedalling, I thought about what had happened and was filled with a great sense of joy and happiness. I had been so consumed by the negativity of social media, I forgot there's a whole heap of people cheering for me. That was a really special moment. To the two women on the bench – thank you for making my day and for sending me that message just when I needed it. It was a reminder to keep on keeping on.

And thank you all for the support you show me. It's never lost on me and gives me the fuel to keep going at times when I may look strong from the outside but internally am not doing so well. I appreciate you all.

To Mum, you will always be my superwoman, my everything. 'Thank you' will never be enough. Even in this book I don't think I've been able to describe the love and admiration I have for you. You are the kindest and purest soul (and please stop worrying about me, I am doing just fine, promise).

Ronnie and Skye, I don't say it aloud enough but I truly love you with all my heart and just pray for you both to be happy and have great times. Know whatever happens in life, I will do all I can to protect, love and care for you.

I believe people come into your life for a reason, whether it's for a short period or a long time. I know there may be people reading this who might feel like I've left them out, and I'm so sorry. To all my closest friends – you know who you are – I love you, I appreciate you, and thank you for just always getting me in all my complexities. The love I feel from you warms my heart, makes me smile. Thank you for being there in person, on the end of the phone, and never allowing me to withdraw in the darkest times. I'm not going to list you all individually because my Gs and my Day 1s will always know that you will forever be my people! I'll throw a little party for us all to celebrate this chapter.

To Edwin Lewis, this whole football journey started with you. The work you've done for kids in east London is everything. Youth workers rarely get the credit they deserve in life but you shaped my future and gave me direction and purpose. You're an angel who guided me from my early years.

To Arsenal Football Club and everyone involved in it, you have been my home and you have my heart always. Through all the ups and downs, the emotions I experienced along the way, I don't know where I would have been without you. From the moment I walked into Highbury Car Park, I knew Arsenal was where I belonged. So many people within the club have played a part in my life and do so to this day. It's a special, unique kind of love and gratitude I have for AFC and I will always be Arsenal, through and through.

To Mr David Dein, who is a special person in my life, guiding me as that father figure. You gave and continue to try and give me a protection I never had. I appreciate the love and care you have for me.

To Louise Sutton and Steve Rudge, the love and respect I have for you both is just mega. You believed in me and supported me from the very start; before agents, before I had a real vision for myself in this broadcasting landscape, you saw something and always wanted me to be me. No matter what happens – because nothing lasts forever – you two will always be so special to me. Thank you for guiding this raw cockney East End girl who would pester you for feedback and advice, Thank you for the honesty always. Thank you for allowing me to trust you both.

I have worked with many people across the BBC – producers, directors, runners, sound, so many areas. I've always understood and appreciated that without everyone's effort from behind the camera, I would never be sitting in front of it being able to do the job that I do and love. It really is one massive team effort; thank you all.

From a very young age, all I ever felt and wanted was someone to believe that I had something to offer and give to this world. Philip Bernie, Charlotte Moore, Barbara Slater, thank you for the belief and support.

There are people I have worked alongside who have helped me and allowed me to grow into the broadcaster I am now, which I am so thankful for. Dan Walker, David Jones, Mark Chapman, Gabby Logan, Clare Balding and Dion Dublin always had a protective arm around me from the get-go. Adam Smith at Sky Sports always gave me the most honest advice, and Billy McGinty saw something in me and created that 'throw to Alex Scott' role on the flagship *Super Sunday* football show. I was then across Sky Sports football as their first ever female contracted regular pundit, which helped change the perspective and narrative: a female pundit for a different diehard audience every weekend. Both BBC and Sky allowed for this change to start happening just by allowing me to be me and trusting I would work as hard as I could not to let anyone down.

To all the teammates, managers and supporting staff I have had over the years, you have all played such a special part in my story and I thank you for the laughter and the tears. To my Boston Breakers family, what a magic three years of my life. To Kelly Smith, thank you for the best gift and lesson I've ever known: how to be vulnerable and learn from heartbreak. And thank you for the best bloody present I've had in my life: MY ELLA.

I've kept my other relationships private and continue to do so. But to my other former loves: cheers to you all. The good, the bad, the ugly – for whatever reason it didn't work, we live and we learn and I wish you all the happiness in the world. I'll say sorry and thanks in one.

Families are complicated things. I know that as a result of writing this book, some of mine will be raging. Others will understand and more yet will have learned things they had no idea about. To Marie, thanks for the selfless act of passing on Nan's ring. That is family love right there. You will never know how much it means to me to have that part of Nan in my life. It took a lot of love inside you to do that. I appreciate you, always. You helped me take Nan home to Jamaica with me.

I've not mentioned stories about Dee in this book but I hope you are reading this and know how thankful I am for you. You saw me grow from a young shy girl who used to come and get her hair styled, cut and cared for, and you helped educate me on my Afro hair when my mum could not. You also helped educate me on Black culture as I continued to grow up in a predominantly white football environment. You were my first ever mentor (before I even knew what that was). You some-how managed to get me to open up and talk and share my life and feelings, and you would offer up advice. I always used to tell you that your chair was therapy for me. You saw me laugh, cry and celebrate achievements and you were my first ever sounding board as I was able to express emotions about my past. Thank you for being you, and I miss you.

Rene . . . I know on the day of this book release you will be up there reading and rejoicing in the fact that this story is finally told. You didn't quite make it for publication day, but we are celebrating your life with a glass of your favourite Irn-Bru right now. You looked after us, you looked after Mum, and we loved you. Thank you.

To Jake Mallen. You were always more than an agent, you were a friend. It felt like a divorce when we parted ways but you hold a special place in my heart. I will never forget the people who helped me get to where I am today, and you were a huge part of that. Thank you.

To Richard, Sara and Alita, thank you for all the day-to-day. Through my highs and my lows, you continue to work to help me see my vision become reality. We are not finished yet, far from it. I am always pushing for more and scared of being in a comfort zone. You three listen, get it, and get me. Thank you.

Finally, to Zennor and Moya, you have allowed me to write this book my way and believed my writing and voice was strong enough. For that, I can't thank you enough. In my head, it was always there and you both guided me to just write. And here we are. Callum Crute, Joanna Taylor, Tim Bainbridge, Anna Cowling, Klara Zak, Natalia Cacciatore and Claire Bush, I appreciate all the work that you have put into this project.

To all the kids who have dreams but feel restricted and held back, this book is for you all. I swear down, if I've managed to get here, and write this book, I promise you can too. It's OK to have big dreams that people around you may think are silly. Go and show them and we'll see who the silly ones are in the end. People ask me what I would tell young Alex if I had the chance. I think, after writing this book, my answer is: nothing. Little Alex, you managed to navigate a lot and you are just where you need to be. Celebrate it.

This chapter is closed now. I'm excited for the next.

Achievements

In most sport books, at the back there is a list of the author's achievements. I am someone that doesn't have my trophies, England caps or awards on show in my house – I'd feel embarrassed if people walked in and saw it all, like it was some sort of shrine to myself (imagine!). Also, I suppose my house is a place where I try to totally switch off from work. The only thing I do have on display is my 100th England cap and the framed shirt to match.

I don't like to talk in depth about my achievements. I remember being asked in an interview how it felt to become the first in this and the first in that and my answer was as follows: I have never set out to be the first in anything, as I honestly believed it may not happen; all I have done is to follow something that I love doing and have a passion for, and the rest is now history. And I feel that this book is so much more about explaining my life and the stories and lessons I took from it than how many trophies and awards I have managed to obtain.

However, thinking about it now as I come to the end of this book and reflect on my life, I am so immensely proud of what I have managed to achieve up to this point. This book has allowed me to take a minute to go,

OH MY BLOODY GOSH. So I am going to celebrate the shiny trophies and awards and write it all here, and this book will take pride of place on my bookshelf at home and I can flick to this page as a reminder that 'Jeeeeez, I did all that'. Maybe I can turn to it in the moments when I need to remind myself that it's OK to give yourself a pat on the back sometimes, to smile and be proud and present in the moment, instead of always thinking, 'What next?'

Awards

MBE for services to women's football

Honorary Doctor of Sport, University of Hertfordshire

Honorary Doctor of Science, University of East London

Honorary Doctor of Arts, Staffordshire University

Broadcasting Press Guild award-winner

Breakthrough award for sports broadcaster for BBC and Sky

FSA Pundit of the Year 2021: the first female to win in this category

Royal Television Society award-winner 2019: Sports presenter, commenter or pundit

Champion of Sport and Wellness award at the Champion of Women Awards

Global Ambassador award from the Football Business Awards

With Arsenal

FA Women's Premier League winner: 2003–4, 2005–6, 2006–7, 2007–8, 2008–9

FA Cup winner: 2003–4, 2005–6, 2006–7, 2007–8, 2012–13, 2013–14, 2015–16

UEFA Women's Champions League Cup: 2006–7

FA Women's Super League winner: 2011, 2012

FA Women's Premier League Cup winner: 2006–7, 2008–9

FA Women's Community Shield: 2006, 2007, 2008

With England

140 caps

FIFA Women's World Cup bronze medal winner 2015

UEFA European Women's Championship silver medal winner 2009

Cyprus Cup winner: 2009, 2013, 2015

With Team GB

London Olympics 2012 quarter-finalist

Media career to date

2016 – *Bear Grylls: Mission Survive* (ITV) winner

2016 – Appearances on *Soccer AM* and *BBC Sport*

2016 – Presenter, London Live

2017 – Presenter, *Match of the Day Kickabout*

2018 – First female pundit across Men's World Cup (BBC)

2018 – First female to appear on *Super Sunday* (Sky Sports)

2019 – First female pundit to appear on BBC's flagship *Match of the Day*

2019 – Co-presenter, *The One Show* (BBC)

2019 – BBC documentary: *England's World Cup Lionesses*

2019 – Women's World Cup pundit (BBC)

2019 – First female footballer to appear on BBC's *Strictly Come Dancing*

2019 – Co-host, *Goals on Sunday* (Sky Sports)

2020 – European Championship pundit (BBC)

2020 – Presenter, *Children in Need* (BBC)

2020 – Presenter, *BBC Sports Personality of the Year*

2021 – BBC documentary: *The Truth About Improving Your Mental Health*

2021 – Commentator, CBS Sports: Champions League

2021 – First female commentator on EA Sports' *FIFA 22*

2021 – Presenter, BBC Olympics coverage

2021 – Presenter of BBC quiz show *The Tournament*

2021 – Presenter, BBC's *Football Focus*

2021 – Presenter, *Soccer Aid* (ITV)

2021 – *Who Do You Think You Are?* (BBC)

2021 – Presenter, *Children in Need* (BBC)

ACHIEVEMENTS

2021 – Presenter, *BBC Sports Personality of the Year*

2022 – Presenter, *The Games* (ITV)

2022 – Presenter, *Soccer Aid* (ITV)

2022 – BBC documentary: *The Rise of Women's Football*

2022 – Presenter of BBC quiz show *The Tournament*

2022 – Presenter and pundit, Women's European Championship

2022 – Presenter, *Children in Need* (BBC)

2022 – Pundit/presenter, Men's World Cup (BBC)

2022 – Author, *How (Not) to be Strong*

Further Support

Refuge is the UK's largest specialist domestic abuse organisation in the UK.

https://refuge.org.uk/

Free 24-hour helpline: 0808 2000 247